View from the Medicine Lodge

Jim Great Elk Waters

SEVEN LOCKS PRESS

Santa Ana, California
Minneapolis, Minnesota
Washington, D.C.

Seven Locks Press
P.O. Box 25689
Santa Ana, CA 92799
(800) 354-5348

Printed in the United States of America

Library of Congress Cataloging-in-Publication Data
is available from the publisher
ISBN 1-931643-05-9

We would like to acknowledge the following for permission to reprint the following materials. (Note: the stories that were ascribed anonymously, are believed to be in the public domain or were written by Jim Great Elk Waters and are not included in this listing. We exercised due diligence but failed to locate the copyright holders of the articles on pages ### ### ###. Please contact us if you are the copyright holders of these items.)

Panther in the Sky. Reprinted by permission of James Alexander Thom ©1989 Ballantine Books

Cover and Interior Design by Sparrow Advertising & Design

What People Are Saying About the *View*

"You created a brilliant picture with your words and touched the depths of my very soul with your vision. You are truly a gifted man. I will read it many times. It is so beautiful, I want to revisit and linger there a while. Thank you for this gift."

> In awe, Leanne Davis
> Writer/Government Representative

"Great Elk, you bring honor to the many areas of your service to humanity."

> Lee Stewart
> Founder, Unity & Diversity

"You're a joy and a blessing to know . When I read your words I see your smile. I send my love to add to your ongoing flow."

> Sedena Mae Conley/Cappanelli
> Native American Producer

"You are one of the most gracious people I know. And I am most grateful for the way you continue to stroll into my life again and again. Peace, my friend."

> Tom Hennessy
> Award Winning Journalist

My Smoke Prayer

In the time when I sat down to write of my People and of their Way, to share this View from my Medicine Lodge, I removed my Pipe from it's pouch and carefully filled it with Sampa grown by our Holy People specifically for Ceremonies.

Taking the Pipe, stem first, I offered the Sampa to the six directions: the east where the sun lives, the south from where we began our long journey home, the west where the sun sleeps, and the north of the Blackness and the cold. I then touched the earth as I offered the pipe to Grandmother Earth, and then reached high to offer it to Grandfather Sky.

I did this as is tradition of my Mide'/Shawandasse People since the beginning of time.

Carefully I lit the Pipe and made my Smoke Prayer, blowing the smoke again to the six directions. This done, I placed the Pipe on some mint. As the smoke curled skyward to carry my Prayer to Creator, I began.

This Smoke I made was to call for a Blessing upon these words and thoughts, that each person who reads from this book will better know the path of the Shawnee Indian today. As is my custom, I gave much thanks for the wisdom that has been shared with me, and for the great Gifts that Creator has bestowed upon my People. And, as always, I asked that if any Sacred words or phrases are read, that they will always be attributed to the Source, Creator, and not to this humble two-legged. I am but the messenger, the conduit for the inspiration.

The Smoke ended and the Prayer for this Blessing was done.

Adean

Now we could begin.

Dedication

This book is dedicated to my best friend and beloved wife, Lolita.

For thirty-eight years, she has been my greatest inspiration, the cause for this book (and anything else I ever thought of doing). Lo was there in the beginning of my path to success and is here beside me now. She is the one who has always said that I am her creative genius, able to accomplish any task, to do it in a right way. It is her reasoned voice that caused me to lose my fear of success.

For that and so very much more, I dedicate this book.

niSooos pëh

Contents

List of Illustrations

About *View From the Medicine Lodge*

I am an okama (a storyteller, or teacher), and it is my job to share with you that which has been shared with me. As we journey together, it is my prayer that I will inspire you, excite you, anger you or in other words, cause you to think. If you think, then you will begin to understand the meaning of this journey. For those who will only read *View* for its enjoyment, that is also good.

I promise that I will not intentionally offend you, but I will tell it as I see it. I will not soft-peddle my passion, and I will not bow to those who would want me to be "politically correct." Not my nature. Know that I use "Indian" and Native American" interchangeably, without malice or disrespect. Accept this, my friends.

As you turn the last page of the last chapter, I pray that I have caused you to experience emotion. That is the mother seed from which grows our comprehension of what it is to truly be "Indian" . . . and that is my job.

The genesis of *Medicine Lodge* was inspired by the many statements and stories from our Elders, of all Indian Nations. Without their wisdom passed through, we are lost spirits in a world of the invaders' descendants. With this understanding, I realized that so many today don't have a clue as to what it means to be Indian, even my own People. In *View from the Medicine Lodge*, I hope to focus, through the reflections of these views, on a wider concept in that regard with its myriad of facets that reflect the individual meanings of being an Indian today. In a documentary I wrote, I refer to this as "not a rehash of history but news at eleven." *View* is that, the American Indian in all our complexity today.

Inspiration

Medicine Lodge's birth occurred at the Ohio Booksellers event in 1995 where I conceived the commitment to create a product that I could also sell there. I spent the day with my tribal brother and sister Sunset Watcher James Alexander Thom and his wife Dark Rain Thom, and Scott Russell Sanders, watching them as they shared their passion for writing with anyone who stopped long enough for them to converse. They are today's storytellers, creating oral traditions onto the talking leaves, the pages of their books. I saw fire in their eyes and felt their obsession. I knew that day that I too was imbued with the sacred emotion of the storyteller. It was their encouragement in those hours spent with their public that caused me to dream of this day.

When I sat down to assemble this collection of thoughts and experiences, I was unabashedly inspired by Mark Hansen and Jack Canfield of *Chicken Soup of the Soul* fame. Their gifts of love have opened many doors for those who are in need. I had originally submitted a manuscript of many of these essays to them for consideration. In the end, Mr. Canfield returned the manuscript with the comment that "although this isn't 'Chicken Soup,' it is a book that must be read."

Megwich

In our language of the ancient Algonquian Speakers, I wish to offer Megwich (my thanks) to the well-source that is so important in the creation of this book.

It is imperative that I honor four important books that were well sources for this inspiration: *Panther in the Sky* and *Children of First Man,* both by James Alexander Thom; *Wisdom Keepers* by Steve Wall and Harvey Arden; and *Through Indian Eyes* by the Reader's Digest Association. I urge you to read these works to feel the fire and wind and water that makes the Spirit of the Indian live. My copies are dog-eared and filled with yellow "stickies," and I use them regularly on my speaking tours.

I want to give a personal thanks to my tribal brother, Chief Hawk Pope, Principal Chief of the Shawnee Nation United Remnant Band (SNURB) for his open sharing of the teachings of his grandparents of the Blue River Community of Shawnee, and for keeping the fires burning. Also, my indebtedness to the Elders of the Shawnee and Blue Creek People.

My thanks to Kenn Kingsbury, Jr., my personal manager and my good friend in good times and bad. Kenn, for the last eight years, has been instrumental in the success of my writing and acting careers. I would also like to thank Timm Severud, creator and publisher of the long-run ezine, *Chautauqua—Echoes in the Wind*. I have included excerpts from his ezine and offer that his work has been pivotal in the *Medicine Lodge's* development.

Without exception, I am proud to offer my profound thanks to my publishers, Jim Riordan and Bud Sperry of Seven Locks Press, who so believed in the value of *View From the Medicine Lodge* that they have added it to their collection of titles.

With this in mind, I have set the following stories and quips to paper for you to share with me, these experience emotions of enjoyment and enlightenment.

Introduction

I am old, and I am very tired now. I think I will sleep for awhile here by the fire to let the flames dance on my eyelids as they help me remember other stories from other times. For an old man like me, The Dreams are so important.

Changing His Feathers
Shawnee Shaman and Storyteller

Being able to share the past is vital to the Storyteller. In the Indian Way, the storyteller is the Keeper of the Wisdom and the Messenger of Enlightenment. Much of this book is based in the spiritual precepts of my American Indian origins.

Often I am asked, "What is the mystique of the Native American? What is the secret to your serenity?" Inwardly, I smile, as I know that much of the time there is no magic and little tranquility in our lives. The fact is we have to deal with all the myriad problems that the rest of you do, coupled with a different philosophical bent. The philosophy will be addressed in the development of this book. The problems? You name it. We have it, too.

Many of these bits and stories are based on the beliefs of the Mide' and Coashellaqua faiths of the Woodland Indians. They are shared freely and are meant to illustrate what I use as guidelines for my life.

In general, we have been taught that we are but a part of Creator's Vision. Not the most important but, in fact, the last creation thought of the Great Spirit. Thus, we must be aware of our position within the

Great Circle of all things living. This thought causes one to truly be more humble.

Why *View From the Medicine Lodge*?

It was plain to me that the purpose of this book was to share some of the ways of how my People bring a better balance to their lives. My driving saying is "Walk in Balance," or strive to perfect our lives while we are here, as best we are able. The ultimate goal is to become the best two-legged or human possible. This is what I believe, that Creator envisioned when He first thought of us, and we became life.

Today's American Indian or Native American or First People, (I forget the current politically correct term, even though I'm one of them), live in a near state of denial. We lost the battles, we lost the wars, but we did not lose our heritage. If tradition is to be a living First People, we must allow it to breathe and grow in the light of today not in the past, the time of the Seasons of the Many Deaths.

12/20   KISE   Chief Hawk Pope

About the Author

My name is, there's the rub sayeth the bard.

Being Indian in modern times is a challenge, particularly in one's nom de plume. In most cases, we have both a given name and a tribal one.

My given name at birth was James Arthur Watters II, continuing the Eurocentric faction of my family's practice of honoring the father. Thus, my first name was a good strong and dignified moniker. In 1980 came name number two. As is the tradition of my Shawnee Tribe, I was given my "adult" name at my Naming Ceremony, held in the august halls of the mobile home kitchen of Crow Woman Knox, our Nation's Mother. Now I was know as Jim Great Elk Watters, another powerful and respectable name.

Then came the Algonquian translation, which was kiji wapiti nappe, Great Elk Waters. Literally, it means the elk's raising its tail and exposing its white rump. "Does this mean I am really Big White Butt?" I queried. Is this my white half? I truly do not think so. (I'm getting confused!)

"Ah, but isn't the word kiji part of the name of the Great Spirit, Kiji Manito?" I asked those present at the ceremony.

Quickly, I set upon the fact that it would just not do to have a name so close to my God's Algonquian name. Fearful for my mortal soul, I have insisted that it be spelled kiji in lower case letters to differentiate the word in a respectful way and that I be called Great Elk. So what happens? Nearly everyone I know calls me kiji.

I quit.

In the late eighties, I went to my parents and asked their permission to make one other change in my name. I wanted to drop the second "t" in Watters. During the days before Indians were named American citizens in 1924, if you were an Indian and were found east of the Mississippi, it was a good bet that you would be removed to the reservations in the west, with only what belongings you could carry. All of your other holdings and properties were to be sold to cover the cost of relocation. It was in that atmosphere that the family bid to hide our "Indian" heritage and assimilate into society. In a bold move, my great grandfather G. T. Watters added (as the story goes), the second "t" in Watters along with the claim that we were descendents of King Michael Watters of County Sligo, the last reigning monarch of Ireland. Who knows? We may indeed be descended from ol' King Michael, but what ever, it stuck.

With their blessing and love, I was at last who I am today, Jim Great Elk Waters.

You should see the reactions of government officials at the DMV, Social Security, and the people at the passport office. Such is the dance of life. Call me anything you wish; just make sure I know you are talking with whoever I am.

Why do I offer all this? To allow you to understand how different it is to be Indian today. The need to hide one's identity is no longer necessary or desirable. As you will see in the stories of the *View from the Medicine Lodge*, our life as Americans is "different." Some good, some not so good, but always different. In any case, I remain your humble servant, whatever the name.

Megwich (thanks).

There is one other bit of confusion in my title. I know "who" I am, but when I'm asked my title, there is another pause. Which title do I use? Today I serve my People of the Shawnee Nation United Remnant Band as their Sub-Chief (a part of the trio of leadership that are elected to be the administration of the tribe) and Buffalo Clan Chief.

The Clan is my familial alliance of the twelve tribal divisions that make up the nation. I am honored to be a Pipe Presenter and Mide' (Spiritual teacher/leader) for my People.

It appears that I must have given up a simple life somewhere along the path. "Is it too late to change?" I question in the recesses of my quiet place. But that would just make another complication in this already long running life of mine.

I have paid my dues.

During 'Nam, I served before the mast at sea as an able bodied seaman aboard wooden hulled minesweepers in the U.S. Navy; was a high steel construction ironworker carrying on the family tradition as a "skywalker" (Its an Indian thing.) I was a volunteer fireman and took my turn in burning buildings and rescues. I was a Cub and Scoutmaster, District Commissioner, and was a founder of several Packs and Troupes. Made custom designed banjo's for Art Gariepy, played stand-up bass in nightclub jazz combos, and painted poster-color seasonal window ads to make a dollar more. Was a printer, design artist and "ad-man" for several companies. Started (and closed) several businesses. Was one of the founders of a little theatre group that still hits the boards today. When mid-life hit, I was driven to return something to society. I work ten years for a mid-sized city in South-central L. A., as a Rehabilitation Specialist, and was on the team that garnered the All-America City award in 1991.

And there was much more.

Amidst all this cacophony, I have found a peace in my Center Place. I am comfortable in this place to which life had guided my presence. I am honored but a bit confused by the many honors bestowed upon this simple country boy from rural Appalachian southern Ohio during the last fifty-eight years.

In the end, I think of myself as a Shawnee Rabbi, a storyteller, a teacher, and a spiritual person who hopes and prays that my meanderings along the Path of Life will help soften the ground beneath the feet of others.

Along the way, I have been honored to work with some truly great people and on so many worthy projects, to which I try to bring authenticity and dignity.

My brother Kepish "Tex" Watters (another skywalker) once said that I was a "Renaissance Man." I prefer to think of myself as a multi-tasking person who lives life with gusto. I have enjoyed working on many film/TV projects such as Disney's *Pocahontas* as Unit Producer, writer, musician, and native voice of "Namontack." I also appeared in many other film and TV projects, including *North, Sioux City, Happily Ever After, How the West Was Won,* and the current issue, *Fear Runs Silent.*

I have been humbled by the tributes bestowed on my screenplays and for my work as a producer/actor. I can hardly take claim though, as I have a great team of creative partners who have contributed their talents to make all this possible. I am in the company of the greatness of the producers Julia Stemock, Kenn Kingsbury, and Ernerst Koeppen; the genius of the writers Steve Karels, Leanne Davis, my brother Kepish Watters, Terryn Barril, and my wife Lolita. The wisdom of my consortium with publicist Norma Foster and world-class artists Ruth Eyrich, and Hawk Pope, and honored composers Bob Christianson and my sister Tula Watters, all bestow their greatness as I view it all from my center of commonness. I think of the process of working with other talent as a form of cloning, the combining of their brilliance to further the success of each project.

We currently have in development so many wonderful projects, including a TV series, a documentary, a musical, a Gothic novel, a children's mystery, and several other extraordinarily interesting undertakings.

I honed my creative skills under the tutelage of the orator Ms. Sade Burns and artist Ms. F. H. D. Crumrine. I was privileged to study at the Dayton Art Institute and under the batons of Professor Harry Smith and Dr. Maurice Reichart. As an artist and musician, I strive to combine the traditional with the contemporary to imbued the works with the spirit of my ancestors, both Indian and Celt. I try to have my art like my writing and poetry, make a statement that draws the you into a journey most uncommon. I humbly offer that these works are hung in galleries internationally.

I am told and believe that the Great Turtle Island, and indeed all the earth and its inhabited creations, have been provided for us so that we may reside in Balance beside our Creator. It is our job to be a proactive partner in the affairs concerning the environment, and in human and animal disquiet. In matters of choice, always make good and right decisions. We need always to strive for balance rather than confrontation.

> As I walk the Red Road, it is with the knowledge that it is not just for Shawandasse . . . but for All My Relations. Therefore, I am dedicated to the reunification of All the Red People and demand the rightful honor and respect that has so long been taken . . . be restored.

I steadfastly believe in the need to demonstrate respect, honor, and dignity and protect the balance of relationships between All Things.

> Like my Shawnee and Fort Ancient ancestors, I have acknowledged my oneness with this ancient homeland. I feel the land as if she were my physical Grandmother, and I am filled with the need to heal and comfort her from the long abuses she has endured. It is our source of life's renewal.

I could not neglect to pay tribute to some of the organizations that have chosen me to lead. First, to my People, the Shawnee, I am honored beyond words to represent you as your Pocili (sub-Chief), Clan Chief, and UN Envoy. I am privileged to serve as a board member and/or officer of the Interfaith Council for the UN, UNA/LA, Allied OhioTribes, eh'dasse, TBInc., and founder of the UNBROKEN CORD. I am tireless in raising awareness and supporting causes like the Optimist, Elks, John Wayne Cancer Institute, Rain Forest Action Network, Sierra Club, and Greenpeace.

It is our job to cause balance in all matters, by recognizing and fulfilling our responsibilities.

For the record, I am an enrolled citizen of the Shawnee Nation United Remnant Band (Roll #A-310) (Ohio HJR-8 1/29/1980).

I am bi-coastal in my residency, if you can count Lake Erie as the "other coast." I have a residence in both the traditional Shawnee homeland in Ohio and California. Lo and I currently have a residence in Lakewood, California.

I met Lo at a USO dance in 1963. She was a widow with three small children. When I met her and her children, I knew that they had been sent a great Gift from *Kiji Manito* to fill a great need. I had been taught that as a *Mide'* I have had several lives to perfect my being as a two-legged, to better prepare me to Pass Over and be with Creator and the Ancestors. When you are in the "last" life, you cannot have children, who by their being would continue your existence in this world and prevent you from Passing Over forever. The Gift of my family has ensured my eventual reunion on the other side of the Veil.

Truth be known, I fell in love with my three children, Steve, Robyn, and Kathy before I finally discovered the wonderful love with Lo. I am so very honored that the children of another man would call me their Dad, and that their mother would have trusted me to fulfill that responsibility. We have been a loving family for thirty-eight years, the kids have grown up, and we now are the proud grandparents to thirteen, and four and one-half great-grandchildren (one in the "oven").

I know that I may have given you more than you ever wanted to know about this person, but I felt that you needed to know a bit about me before you read this book. In doing so, you just might get a feel for how I view the Medicine Lodge.

1   Tomorrow's Contemplation on Today

These days people seek knowledge, not wisdom. Knowledge is of the past, wisdom is of the future.

Vernon Cooper, Lumbee Elder

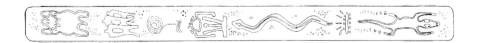

Grandmother Turtle

It is told to us by the Ancestors in our oral traditions, that when we seek knowledge to see the important things, we must go on a quest, a spiritual search, to walk on the other side of the web of life. This long-held tradition has always been our greatest guidance to wisdom.

In the oral tradition of my People, the Shawnee I would like to help you understand our relationship to the land and our first quest story, of our Grandmother, the earth.

A long time ago, in the time of our first grandfathers and our grandmothers (yes, we too have grandmothers), before there were the two-legged humans, before Tula the earth existed, there was only water. Everywhere as far as one could see there was only water. Swimming in that great sea were all the People, the birds, and the animals.

One day a voice cried out, "Oh great Creator, we are very tired of swimming. Why is there no place to rest? Could you please give us a place to lay upon?"

And the voice of Creator spoke: "Why have you not asked before? I have been waiting. I will help you make your place to rest." Creator continued, "At the bottom of the water, there is much mud where the great Tula Geah, the Earth Mother, lives. If one of you will bring back a piece of the Earth mud, I will make a place for you to rest," and the Voice was silent.

So all the People decided that someone should dive to the bottom for a piece of the mud. Then they would have a place to stand or lay.

Old Grandmother Turtle, in her crackled, way said, "I will do it!" And in unison, all the People said, "Oh no, Grandmother, one of the younger people will do it. You are too old."

> The power of
> need always
> exceeds the fear
> of trying.

First was the duck. "I can do it," he said as he took a big breath and dove. Down, down, down he went, and up, up, up he came. "Where is the mud? Did you find the mud?" And he answered, short of breath, no."

Grandmother Turtle again volunteered. And all repeated, "You are too old."

Each of the people in turn tried. Taking even bigger breathes of air, they went ever deeper, down, down, down. And up, up, up, with no mud.

Each time Grandmother would say, "But I can do it." Finally, all had tried. And now because they were all exhausted from their futile attempts and desperately wanted a place to lay, they finally agreed, "Alright Grandmother, you try."

First, she took a really big breath, and because she was wise, she took another even bigger breath. With a splash, she dove down, down, down . . . down, down, down. Until they could no longer see her shadow in the water. She had been under for a very long time now, and all the People knew she had drowned. And they were sad.

Then bubbles slowly began to appear. Bluup. Bluup bluup, bluup bluup bluup. Suddenly, there was a great commotion in the water. Deep in the cobalt blue they saw the shape of the old turtle. She was rising, up, up, up; and at last she broke the surface with a great gulp for air.

On her shell was a piece of mud. Instantly, keeping His promise Creator made much land from the Tula on the shell of the old turtle. Now all the People had a place to rest. All the people were very happy. And Grandmother Turtle was the happiest of all. The oldest of them all had caused the gift of Tula for the young not yet born from the land, that had been brought from the depths.

The next time you see a turtle, look at her shell. You will see it is all fractured, cracked from the weight of carrying the world on her back. Then you will remember the time when this storyteller told you of the creation of Tula, the land we call earth. It is my job to tell you of these things. It is my job to help you understand our connection with all that is in and about us. Aden, it is done.

Been Trying

In Indian Country things are much the same as in your home town. We do like things you and have similar feelings. A modern Indian is hard to identify from any other American. Despite all our differences, we are a part of the fabric of this society.

With that said, here is a story that could happen anywhere. It just happens to be about an Indian family.

Still chewing on the same bit of bacon he had been working on for the last few minutes. "Well," he says as we sat at the window in Jennie's Diner, "do you think that Harry'll get his barley before the wet sets in?"

"Spit that danged rind out, Pa, and listen to me. This is real important," I says, as he puts his napkin to his mouth and discreetly removes the piece of pig skin.

"The dean over at Bellwhist, they say, is looking to fill the Psych 104 spot next period. Mentioned your name, I did," he says.

"Pa, I can speak for myself, and anyway I can't afford to work for those wages in this day's world. Now would you please listen, for just a minute? Please!" I nearly shouted.

Surprised myself, and Pa gave me one of those patented glances that he used to throw when I was a kid. Heck, I'm twenty-four now, a college grad, with dry ears, and he still makes me feel worthless. He's done that to me near all my life. Seems I'll never measure up to HIS expectations.

Oh yes, he puts on those airs with his suit and tie, using his hanky and all, but everyone knows he's just a dirt farmer. A danged redneck plow jockey. And he acts so proud.

Then he says, "So what's put the fire in your forge now?" he says, and starts chewing on another piece of slab bacon. "Just love this taste," he says.

"Well?" he says.

"Well, what?" I says.

"What is so important that you 'please' to tell me?" he says.

"I've been trying to tell you that."

"Tell me what?" he interrupts. God, he infuriates me when he does that!

"I've been trying to tell you that ol' Mr. Jacobs, the Constable, is writing you a ticket on that worthless wreck of a F-100 pickup."

"Looky there, he's sticking it in the window right now," I says.

"Oh that," he says.

And I'm puzzled, as Pa is known to be as tight as a bolt on a bank vault.

"Pa, that'll cost you plenty," I says, looking back at ol' eagle eyes Jacobs. God, has he cost me a bundle over the years, I think, and turn to see Pa sipping his coffee.

"I will never understand you if I live to be,"

"Hush boy," he says abruptly. "You'll soon understand." Looking first at the window and then directly at me, he says, "I'm going away, and you will have to look after things."

"Going where, when, why?" I near well shout. I pause "You didn't tell me you were going,"

"Sush boy, calm down," he says. "Been going to tell you, but I didn't have all the information. Guess I do now tho'," he says. "I'm going to die, soon," he says matter-of-factly.

"What?" Stones pound my head as I try to understand what he has just said.

"Gonna be OK. I mean that you are gonna to be OK," he continues. "Been dying from the cancer for some time, but didn't know how long I'd have."

"Cancer?" I say in disbelief, as horror images of that dreaded disease race through my memory.

"Prostrate," he wrongly intones as if he'd said butter or something. He continues, "That's why I sent you to that big school upstate, to fill your head with all the things I never had the chance to learn."

"But, Pa, prostate cancer will,"

"Doc told me he would send the word today." He stirs his coffee a bit. "If it was good, he'd have brought it his self." Puts the spoon neatly on his napkin. "Bad, well, Jacobs was to put the report in ma' truck."

He stops, not moving at all, just looking out the window at the truck for the longest time.

"I didn't know, Papa." I says. "Can I, ?"

My whole world's spinning in on me now.

"You already have," he says. "In our family, no one's ever been more schooled than you, and with good common sense to boot," he says. "No sir, son, you done it all, already." He pauses to look out the window again. As he looks back, I see a tear run down his cheek. Papa never cried.

"Our ancestors prayed for the Cord from the first parents to remain unbroken." He gazed deep into my eyes until I felt he was square in my heart. "You're the future they envisioned, and mine, the family's reason for being. You are our future," he says with open pride.

He stops and takes out his handkerchief, wipes at his eyes and says, "Now eat your eggs, a'for they get cold, as if they ain't already."

I Recall

I recall the memories from those days when all meat was juicy and tender, and no game was too swift for a hunter. When I was young, every day was a beginning of some new thing, and every evening ended with the glow of the next day's dawn.

Ivaluarjuk Iglulik, elder
From *Through Indian Eyes*

Miracles in Commonness

You call it wild, but it wasn't really wild, it was free.
Animals aren't wild, they're free.

Leon Shenandoah, Onondaga

In my special garden enclosure awash in spring colors nearly thundering with joy, I sit encompassed, peace bound. I am surrounded by flamingo walls and patio pavers and carpets of grass that feel firm, while roses and tomatoes young and tendriled beans, reach skyward. They extend in crescendo as a chorus paying homage to the center of this tiny universe, the grand giant tree that is my dark green roof encircled in cerulean blue, in cityscape a hundred miles square, on a grand boulevard constant with traffic mirroring the grey-black ribbons that freeway all about not four miles away.

I have determined my morning refuge.

Here, with strong coffee and morning newsprint, I sit to ponder life anew this day. As I scan each word and illustration, I am imperceptibly distracted, first by slow-learned awareness that the sounds of man have been replaced, or more appropriately, have been overwhelmed by a tiny bird's voice, and another, and another until the very air that surrounds me is filled with a bewilderment of melodies.

They speak and serenade one another in constant joy, seeking mates and chastising others fluttering too near. The brilliance of their sounds combined, overwhelm the urban cacophony and cause it to be transformed as if by plan, into a bucolic meadow, far in the countryside of my distant youth.

Here in this place, I am alone in a dream-meadow, filled with undomesticated garden visitors of now, and sepia sounds and greyed images from times long ago. Here in this place, for the moment, I exist in the combined best of realities. Here I accomplish what others futilely seek as they plod about, encased in the fabrications of daily routine.

I am as fascinated this morning, as I was in childhood, by the daring acrobatics of house wrens darting through the oleander thicket and elm tree, held mesmerized by conversations between dove and mate in echoed melody. Orchestrated rhythms of countless anteceded coveys in the dance of life eternal, continuing.

The magic of these angel-like beings, flying without prescribed direction or necessity, must please today, at this exact moment, the Creation Source, just as it did the first time He saw them in His thoughts and they became that which they are. Feathers, red and yellow and brown and grey, against the bottomless blue of sky and verdant green of giant trees, reflect their sister world of plant people in color, play against grass green and earthen-toned garden soil.

Yes, this is true magic gifted to those who will but pause to observe this constant in a world of needless change. I am the artist taunted to re-create in medium this sphere which is all about. I am the country child in wide-eyed wonderment, filled with inherent knowledge, understanding that only Creator can master such things.

Yet I am challenged by that same Creator to attempt to replicate this work. Striving for perfection in all things, for perfect balance in life, is a part of the creation, is the path of fulfillment to be walked if one is to be allowed one day to join the

> **Close with familiarity the complexities of life, one soon loses sight of the magic that is simplicity.**

ancestors beyond the veil. Such are the miracles in commonness that fill my garden, that place of momentary escape.

Sipping coffee now cold, to sounds of tires on pavement and engines roaring against inertia, the smell of it all permeates my special garden place once more.

I rise and exit into a make-believe place of urbanity, where once again I try to create balance.

It's my purpose here.

Have by Love

Why should you take by force that from which you can have by love? Why should you destroy us, who have provided you with food? What can you get by war?

I am not so simple as not to know it is better to eat good meat, lie well, and sleep quietly with my women and children. To laugh and be merry with the English and be their friend. To have copper hatchets and whatever else I want, than to fly from all, to lie cold in the woods and to be so hunted that I cannot rest, eat, or sleep.

Anonymous
From *Through Indian Eyes*,
with comments by kiji wapiti nappe.

A child's embrace, a grandmother's grace, are gifts beyond purchase.

Cry Not For My Father

For nearly all this century, my father, Chief Ten Moons Watters, was filled with the greatness of change that has occurred. He spoke often of his fascination of having been born in the horse and buggy days and paddle wheelers of his Ohio River region, and with the wonder of scientific discoveries and societies' evolution since.

From the dust of the dirt trail he walked to Turtle Mountain to the precious materials from the moon brought home by his modern heroes, he was charged with its wonder. Telephones, radios, and television enchanted him. He learned how they worked, tearing them apart and reassembling them to function once more. He marveled at the explosion of communication and education. He was awed at the way the world had become small, how one could go to the far corners of the earth in but a matter of hours. The span of his life must have been truly spectacular.

Through all this, he had ridden two horses—one red and the other white—across the breadth of this time. One based in the tradition and honor of his Indian ancestors, and the other charged with his European/American forefathers' never-ending quest for the new. Mounted with a foot firmly planted on the back of each, he kept his balance throughout.

My father made no compromise. The world of his youth, rooted in history and tradition, had to accept the challenge and attune to the "unbelievable changes that have occurred" in his lifetime.

This is the story of the closing of this chapter of his life and the unfolding dawn of his tomorrow, where he has returned to the innocence and magic of his youth.

As the Shawnee Buffalo Clan gathered on the top of the hill around the freshly dug hole in the sand, it was a one last time for remembrance. We had carried the body of our father, first by caravan to this outlook above the Ohio River, and now by hand to this burial place where so many of our ancestors had been lain.

It had turned grey and icy in the valley the Iroquois named Ohio, the "Beautiful Place." Sleet driven hard by the bitter cold winds of the First Snow Moon cut our flesh, reminding those gathered that we had not yet begun our final journey.

The Elders, bundled in heavy coats and blankets, turned their backs to the frigid breath of the approaching storm. Their understanding of this time sent a gentle comfort that warmed the warriors, men and women, as they placed the box on the cross members.

Our salt tears froze upon our cheeks and rushed with the sleet to the sand. It was now time to send this great Chief, the Elder of all Ohio Shawnee, to the place of his ancestors. It was time to say tanakia, farewell until our paths cross again.

Each of his Tribe, his Clan, his children and friends, offered in their own way, their final rites according to their faith. Born of Christian parents, this son of Chief Big Dad and Ma Jessie received first, the final benedictions of that faith. Then the last rite of a 32nd Degree Mason. Next Tula Nappe, his elder daughter, offered prayers of her faith the, Bahai, and the others in silence said their parting prayers.

At last the Medicine Way Speaker, with a feathered prayer stick in hand, symbolic of the Coashellaqua ancient beliefs of the Shawnee, faced the east. In a booming voice that echoed off the hills of Ten Moons' youth, the Speaker cried out: "Wee-lo! Wee-lo! Wee-lo! We send you our Great Chief." To the south, again three times, he cried out and said, "We send you our beloved friend."

Looking into the west, down the long grey ribbon of river where the old Chief and his mother had often contemplated days' end, the shaman offered: "We send you our cherished father." Once more he turned. Now to the north the sound reverberated deep into the ancient hills as he spoke those sacred words a last time.

"Wee-lo! Wee-lo! Wee-lo! We give you the care of your brother Chief Ten Moons," and they echoed into chilled silence. The ceremonies had concluded.

It was his way through life that the important things be properly attended. One could but smile at the thought that even during this time he had "covered all his bases."

The tears had dried and the cold again cut hard as the reality of the moment returned with the bitter winter winds to these Woodland People. Yes, it was a time to remember, a time to recall our Shawandasse Babackis'iganatuk-Okema Metathwe Dekeelswa, (Shawnee Elder-Chief Ten Moons).

He was born just thirty miles east of that knoll on October 30th, four years into this century and in the last days of the Harvest Moon. He had seen his world change from wagons and horses, buffalo and elk, to an environment he could never have dreamed.

His last recollections in this life were of his earliest times. He recalled his first school, the Turtle Mountain Territorial School, and the trip there by covered wagon. He remembered the remnants of the great herds of buffalo and the first motorcar he encountered. He told stories of the hard but honest life of his youth; and spoke always of his father and mother, his brother, and all their friends now long gone.

For nearly as many seasons as days in the year, he had walked on his cherished Grandmother Earth. He had poured his cup to the brim and had filled his being with the grandness of life. His love touched so many and his gentle leadership had enriched all who knew him.

But he was the last of his generation. He was his own "Ishi." No longer could anyone reminisce the glory of his youth, and he missed that, to the center of his being. The Tribe and the Clan of his time were gone. And now it was his time to join All His Relations.

He closed his eyes to this place just hours after he had marked his eighty-eighth year. He passed through with the First Snow Moon of the ninety-second year of his century. It had been a grand adventure.

To his friends and loved ones, I ask you to consider these thoughts. Cry not for my Akotha, Ten Moons, for my Father has at last gone home to All

> He lived well and full the measure met, to have outlived his chums was his only regret.

His Relations. Our predecessor faced death with the wisdom that strength comes from the ancient ones at these times. Death is not to be feared nor welcomed but is simply the last step of life on this side of the veil.

When we take our last breath from Grandfather Sky and rest our body upon Grandmother Earth's breast, our life, that spirit which makes us eternal, steps through the web of the ancient spider. Then at last we can walk with All Our Relations.

Yes, my nekahs, my friends, find joy in the memory of Chief Ten Moons, for that was his gift to you. Think of his presence as he would rest wrapped in a blanket at the entry to the ceremonial Great House. Remember the spirit that fills your being each time an Elder celebrates the Sacred Rites with our People.

Do not feel the pain of sorrow, for the Good Great Chief Ten Moons never gave you sorrow. But remember him at Red Fox Camp and Shawandasse as he sat in the shade of the trees, telling stories of another time to our children, of a time when he was the child.

He made the four-day journey from two-legged to spirit with his Kindewa Chena Meswammi Pitchkosan (his Eagle feathers and Sacred Treasures). The People, his family and friends, were ever vigilant and on the fourth day, he was lain among the bones of his Clan.

Now in the cool embrace of Grandmother Earth, with his first daughter near his head, his parents as always share the south wind from the hills below. With his warrior brother at his side, the remains of this great Shawnee Chief will make the passage from flesh to dust. That is, as is should be, the completion of the two-legged's Mortal Circle.

No, my friend, do not feel the bitterness of despair with the absence of our Brother Chief Ten Moons, Okema Metathwe Dekeeklswa. But sing often our songs of happiness, for his life was a most happy one. And tell the stories he imparted to you, for that should be his greatest remembrance.

His gift was from the ancestors, our unchanged sacred oral tradition. The remembered word, the spoken history throughout the hundreds of generations is the living reality of All Our Relations.

2 Our Deep Roots

Love is the cord that binds the family soul.

Kiji

As great oaks tap

Grandmother

Earth's mystic

powers, we must

listen for the

Elders and their

earned wisdom.

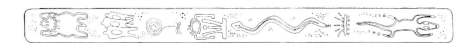

The Boy and the Snake

This story is told in the lodges for the first people around the world since time began. Its message is clear.

I have taken the liberty of sharing the teaching tool in this modern narrative manner rather than in the stoic traditional form. Both are important; however, my Mide' taught me in this form. The best way to understand this is to compare the stories in the Torah, the King James version of the Bible and the Bibles published in today's dialects. The words change, but the stories remain solid and are valid teaching tools in every format.

A long time ago, in the time of our Grandparents' Grandparents there was a young Mide' boy who was most trusting. He accepted that which anyone told him as truth for he had never been told a lie by anyone in his Circle of Life. All those who lived in his village of great mounds and lodges, loved and protected him. Although he was on his path to manhood, he had not yet learned of those who are different from his people.

It was during this time that he was counseled by the Elders and the leaders of the Men's Council and the grandmothers of the Women's Council. Here he learned much about the history of his People and of the long trail they had traveled from the First Parents Circle. At their feet, he sat and heard their many stories. They told him of all that was good and of Matchemonito, the Evil One, who would trick you with his stories. They all told him to learn to know the difference between that evil and the good that surrounded him.

It was here that he was also assigned to his Mide', his personal teacher, who would teach him of the four levels of the earth and sky. It was in this time that he was sent on his many Quests of Solitude where he was to meditate on the teachings he had so far received.

On one beautiful spring day, while he was preparing for this Mide'way manhood path by fasting alone, he had wandered into the forest far from the village of the many smokes. He had built a good fire in this camp place and had become engrossed in reflection on what had been taught him by his mentors. He was not aware that a visitor approached. It was his Mide'.

"Why do you sit here in thought when you are needed up there?" asked the old man as he pointed to a cave in the side of the cliff nearby. "Did I not tell you to discover everything about the levels of the earth," he continued, "and is not the cave a part of that earth?"

"Yes, Mide'," said the boy, quickly standing with head bowed to honor the Mide'. "I was thinking of the many lessons you have taught me, my Mide'," the boy stammered.

"Yes, boy, I understand, but now is a time of action, of exploration of those lessons well remembered," the old man stated. Then pointing to a small dark spot high up the nearby cliff, he said, "Go to that cave and when you return to our village, tell me what you have learned." With that, the old man turned and walked back toward the village.

The boy knew that there would be no other explanation of his task so he immediately set out towards the cave and began the ascent towards its black mouth high above.

He slipped on the loose stone debris at the base of the cliff and stumbled on up to the solid rock wall. The climb was hard and there were few places to grab the cold sharp stone wall with his little fingers and fewer places for his toes to find, but he finally reached the cave.

It was dark inside, and a cold wind blew from its innards. He thought, "This cave must be open to the great wall of ice that is far to the north where the wind blows cold and wet year round." He was afraid to enter the cave. That was normal; as he would later learn, even grown warriors did not cherish the idea of entering that cave.

At last he drew his courage and entered the cave a few feet. He waited for his eyes to adjust to the darkness. Soon he was able to better see the interior of the cave. It was very cold now and he could see icicles hanging from the top of the cave's maw. He shivered. In the distant gloom, he was able to make out a stone bridge across a deep chasm.

Walking to the stone platform, he crossed the bridge.

The filtered light shimmered on the wall ahead. He thought he saw something strange in the ice that hung in sheets from above. Moving closer, he peered intently. Laying among the icicles was a water moccasin, a most poisonous snake. The serpent who was usually a gold and brown color was now blue from the cold.

"A blue snake? How curious," thought the boy.

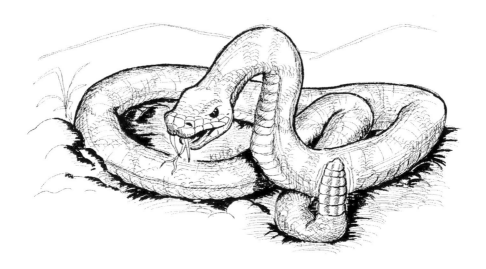

The snake moved its yellow eyes set into the blue flesh and looked up. "Man-boy," he whispered, "I am very cold. My body is frozen and I cannot move," the snake said. His voice was like crystals shattering in the cold air. "Will you help me?"

The boy hesitated. After all, it was a strange snake. But he had been told of this snake and its and venom. Even though this moc was frozen stiff, he was still dangerous.

"I am frozen and cannot move," the snake continued. "Hold me close to your warm flesh and carry me back to your campfire where I may warm myself and be on my way." As an added thought, the snake offered, "That is all I want, thank you."

The boy looked at the snake and respectfully lowered his head, never taking his eyes off the serpent's eyes. "I cannot help you," he said. "You are a dangerous snake that can kill me with your evil bite as surely as we speak. If I take you to my fire, you will bite me, and I will die and never see my people again."

The snake looked away and said with a humble voice, "That is not true man-boy. I am honor-bound that I will not bite you if you help me."

The boy still refused. "You are the great water moccasin. You are crafty and you lure your prey with your yellow eyes, and I am told that you do not always speak the truth," the boy said with a stern voice.

> There can never be true trust of one who would have your all, for with that trust you will grant that desire.

"Yes, my friend, in most situations you would be right," the snake said. "But I am trapped in this icy grave. If you help me, I will be honor-bound not to bite you."

The snake grew silent. His yellow eyes no longer moved back and forth as they had done before.

Nothing moved.

The boy thought of all the teachings of his Elders and of the Women's Council and the Men's Council and of his Mide'. They had all taught him to be kind and loving and to help the less fortunate. Yes, they did warn him again and again of the Evil One.

"But even the Evil One needs help, too," he thought. "I cannot just let him die, frozen forever in this icy grave place."

Time passed and he still meditated.

"Just this once will I be able to trust him?" he wondered. "Even the Evil One can appreciate the gift of his life and will spare me," he reasoned.

Finally, the boy, fearing that the snake may truly die in the cold, and feeling sympathy for the snake's plight, bent down and picked the frozen snake from among the icicles.

He put the ice-covered snake inside his shirt and descended the perilous face of the cliff, searching for the places he used earlier in his climb. At last he reached the bottom and hurried back to his camp and the warmth of the fire.

As he reached the still burning campfire, he gently removed the snake from his clothing, bent down and tenderly lay its motionless body by the fire.

Before he could stand back up, the snake struck out.

The boy cried out in pain and regret. "You promised if I brought you here, you would not bite me!" he stammered in disbelief.

The snake coiled up, raised his head and stated, "I appreciate that you have saved my life and I regret that you will soon die, but you knew who I was when you picked me up," the snake said as it slithered away.

The boy dropped to his knees, feeling the fire of the venom as it flowed through him. His flesh and bone now ached from the poison as he watched the snake disappear into the scrub of the forest. His eyelids lowered and the light dimmed as he thought, "How tired I am now that I am dying." Now he could only feel the breeze as it brought the familiar smells of the forest he so loved. In that same light wind he could smell the smoke from the fires of his home, then, there was only darkness. The boy would never again see his beloved People, hear of their great wisdom, or walk upon the great mound village of the many smokes.

That is the end of the story.

In this day of great promise and good life, we still encounter Matchemonito in his deceptions. See him in the drugs, alcohol, or anything else of that nature. See him in the violence, crime, or perhaps even those we would want to love. See him in those who would make us other than we are, and cause us to lose it all.

As you are faced with such things, no matter how enticing they may seem, remember that you may never again see the forest or enjoy its smells, or smell the smokes from the great mound village of the many smokes, as you hear him say . . .

"You knew what I was when you picked me up . . . "

Beyond History

We have lived upon this land from days beyond history's records, far past any living memory, deep into the time of the legend. The story of my people and the story of this place are one single story. We are always joined together.

Pueblo Elder
From *Through Indian Eyes*

Then There was Light on the Bundle

In the days of Cornstalk and Tecumseh, each Shawnee village and town had a Great Council Lodge for the People to meet and solve the problems of the time. Council was important to these People who lived in a Chief Way Democracy, for here each person had a voice, and each voice was important.

Then people not from the Great Turtle Island came, and there were wars. For two hundred years, the People were pushed deeper into the woodlands, until at last there was no place for the invaders to push them.

After the People had been taken in chains to the lands in the sun-set, after the last fires of the last of the many great Shawandasse towns and villages had grown cold and the name of this People was no longer spoken, we still came together in Council.

At first, the keepers of the Great Meswammi, the Nations Bundle, met deep in the forest. Here, far from the eyes of the new strangers in our ancient land, they kept the Council.

> **The mystery of all things Sacred are reminders to us as we once again open the Bundle.**

As the woods gave way to the iron plow blade, the People that had stayed behind to keep watch over the graves of our Grandfathers' Grandfathers, finally rested. Council was held in barns and tobacco sheds and in the Long-knives' lodges where they now lived.

Tens of years passed, and the People held these secret councils away from the eyes of the ever-multiplying "territory settlers." Each year, it became more difficult to find a safe place to hold Council.

Finally, the pressure of the new ways, the strange new "houses," the plow that split open Grandmother's breast, the invaders' indoor schools, and new religion had taken the People away from the power of the old ways. No longer did the People come to their Shawandasse leaders for guidance. No longer did the People hold Council.

In the darkness of a shed, his face stained with the bitter tears of defeat, the Kitch Okema, the Great Chief of the People, gently nailed the Nations' singular treasure to the wood. Filled with the pain of failure, he placed The Bundle between the walls. With boards, he entombed the sacred hiding place and slowly turned and walked through the door.

The Chief, by this last act, had hoped that the ancient relics of ten thousand councils might be saved for a few years from the pot-hunters and museums. There would be no more Council. The Shawnee's place between Grandfather Sky and Grandmother Earth was gone

Under the mark of the second great war of the Great White Father's world, a male child was born to that old Chief's son. This child was to once again pick up the sacred fire stick of the Shawandasse and lead its People in the ways of their Grandfathers. Thick Water would be proud of this great grandson, the man called Tukemas, Hawk at the Setting Sun.

At the hand of his grandfather, the young Tukemas watched and listened as the old man taught him the Ways. Daily he would learn more of the things of a thousand generations gone before. At times he felt that his head would burst simply from the volume of words that Grandfather told him.

Years passed as he learned even more and he practiced those instructions daily. It was now his time to lead. With trembling hands, this young man took the Nation's Bundle from the old Chief. Now there was light again on the center of the People.

Once again we held Council.

This was over forty summers ago, more than sixty Councils. We have held Council in fields and woods, in homes, and in community buildings. We have held Council on the land of friends.

Now, after nearly 200 years of no home, we have our own land. As did our Grandfathers' Grandfathers, we too will now hold Council in the old way. First, the Council was held in the open upon this sacred land. Then, we too had a Great Council Lodge in which to assemble, for with the help of our true friends, we have this new Lodge, this returned land.

Tecumseh's Shawnee Creed

Do not kill or injure your neighbor,

for it is not him you injure . . .

you injure yourself.

But do good to him,

therefore add to his days of happiness,

as you add to your own.

Do not wrong or hate your neighbor,

for it is not him you wrong,

you wrong yourself.

But love him for Manito loves him,

As He also loves you.

Words ageless,

crafted from

passion, recall

again the cause

of civilized

people.

The First Encounter

As recalled from the stories of the oral tradition, told to Great Elk as a child by his Shawnee Mide' grandaunt Jean Price, and confirmed as a part of our oral tradition later by Shawnee Elder Brown Bear . . .

There are many stories to be told about these things and these times. Maybe we should start back at the beginning. We start in the time of the First Encounter, not the Creation. This is the story as it was told to me. I was instructed to pass it on, as is our oral tradition.

In the time of our Grandfathers' Grandfathers, a long time ago, this story came about around the time when the land was getting colder. This time it came about when our Ppeople would walk to where the great white bear lived, and we would go to this place in the cold north every summertime. We went to this place to gather fish and to dry the water on the land to make salt so we could take it back across the Spaylaywitheepi to the warmth of the winter to the south.

These were good times for our people. We were not at war and we had not known war. This was before the time that man thought they should have the right to take something that others have by force. This was indeed a good time.

As we were camped in our summer camp along this great body of water, one early morning we awoke as a group of people were coming out of the cold of the north. They were walking into the morning sun. They were a strange people who spoke not our language and their appearance was different. Their eyes pointed to the stars and their skin was as burnished copper.

We could see as they came to our camp that they were tired and hungry and there was sickness in them; they needed a place to rest, and they needed food. So our people gave them places in our lodges and we gave them our food and we warmed water and we warmed their bodies and we put furs and blankets upon those that had little cover and we put moccasins upon the feet of those who had none.

We listened to their strange language and did not understand what they were saying. Some of our wise old men and women, our Shaman, our Chiefs, sat down with their old wise people and after a time, they were able to understand something about these strange people.

Their story was very sad, for it was a tragedy you see.

In the time of their Grandfathers' Grandfathers, there had come a great famine upon their land, a drought, where the four-leggeds and Feathered People no longer existed. The creeks dried up and there was no place for the Finned People, and they died. The tree people turned brown, the grass people blew away, and the dust was there, at once and everywhere.

And they went to a great holy man, and this two-legged set out to the place where the great prayers were given. When he returned, he possessed an important message for all.

"Walk out into the morning sun and at last you will come to the end of the Great Turtle Island, where you will find good food and water. And you will find the animal people; and you will find a place for you."

These people did as their Shaman/Medicine Man—this great holy man of good vision—told them. They gathered together their belongings and walked into the morning sun, away from their land forever.

They walked, and their children grew to be men and women, and their old people died and were buried along the trail. New generations were born and grew old. At last, they came to the edge of the Great Turtle Island.

Indeed it was green and there was fresh food and water. This was good. But the famine and the drought followed. So they walked along the edge of the endless water. As they walked these many days, these many moons, these many seasons, since their Grandfathers'

Grandfathers told them to leave, the air got colder and there was much more of the white snow.

Soon there was no green, only snow and ice, and they continued to walk along the edge of the land into the morning sun. Many thought this would be the end of all the People because they did not know what they could eat. But there was good food there. There was food in the water and food on the land.

Now, too, they had the great white bear with its long teeth, that lived in the water. It would come out of the water, and they would kill it with their spears. The food was good to eat, and they used the fat to make fuel to keep them warm. They melted the snow and ice, and they had water.

So they continued to walk where it was cold, into the morning sun.

At last the day came when they must make a decision, for if they continued to walk along the edge of the Great Turtle Island, they would be walking away from the morning sun. They knew that for all these years, the morning sun had provided for them and had taken care of them. So they decided to continue into the morning sun and away from the water.

They walked a long time. Many of the people died and again the children became old men. The children's children continued to walk, until at last they walked into our camp that one morning and we fed them. And we learned this sad story from them.

After a while, we learned to speak their language and they learned to speak our language. We came to know that these were good people, and we invited them to stay with us and help us catch fish. Ah, they were good fisher people. They knew the way of catching fish the new way, with things we know now as nets. These nets caught many more fish than the spear we used, and this was good.

Then the air began to grow colder, the days were shorter, the nights were long, and we knew that soon we must walk away to our summer place across the great Spalawathepe, across the great Kentuck', the hunting ground of the people, to our place where our people have lived.

But it was strange about this river, my friends, because when this all took place, the Spalawathepe did not run like it does today. The mighty stream flowed to the place of the cold, from the warmth of the mountains, not from the morning sun to the evening sun as it does now.

And this time, as we walked toward and came to the great river, these new people said, "Let us make camp; we must make a decision again." They sat and made council and after a long time, with much thought, they came to a decision. "If we continue our journey as we were when we came into your camp, into the morning sun, what will we find, my brothers?"

Our leaders, our great Chiefs, told them, that "If you walk into the morning sun, at last you will come to the end of the great island.

There you will find good food, sweet water, and much game. You could put your canoe into the edge of this great body and go out into this water; but if you go beyond the sight of the land, you will never return. For no man has gone beyond the sight of the Great Turtle Island and returned."

They thought about this. They held Council and asked us: "But if we walk the way we are now, toward the warmth, not the setting sun, what will we find?" Our Kitch Okema told them that after a while they would cross the area known as the great Kentuck', our hunting area, and they would come to a mountain and then, at last, to the edge of the land.

"There again, it is the same as the edge of the Great Turtle Island where the morning sun comes. Do not go beyond the sight of the land because you will never come back."

Then they said, "We do not want to go back to the cold, the direction from which we came. But there is one more direction we must know about. If we were to walk into the direction of the setting sun, into the warmth instead of the cold, what would we find?"

Our chiefs told them a great story of a great plain of land where there were many animals, the shaggy buffalo, the bear, the elk, the deer, the rabbit, squirrels. Grass was as high as a man's shoulder, the water was sweet and cool, and the land was good . . . and the land was where it should be, a good place to live.At the edge of this land was a great barrier mountain, which no man had passed across and lived to tell what was on the other side.

So they went back into Council and thought long. They prayed and at last they came to us and said: "My brothers and sisters, you have been good to us. You have given us a home, food, shelter, and clothing, but above all, you have given us a part of yourselves, your love, your respect. For this, we could never repay you."

"But a decision has been made by our people that we will part our ways here. It is decided that we will move into the setting sun, we will cross that plain, we will go to that great mountain barrier and cross it. We will send someone back to tell you what is on the other side of that great barrier."

So the next morning, when the sun rose from where it sleeps overnight and warmed our camp, we saw that our friends had packed all their clothing, their lodges, and were ready for a long journey. They came to us and spoke of the desire of some of their people to stay with us. We welcomed them and said they were our brothers and sisters. Some of our people, who had come to love these people very much, requested to go with them. We bid them good health and prayed that Creator would always be with them.

They parted that day, walking into the place where the sun goes to sleep, promising they would cross that great mountain barrier and send someone back to tell us what is there.

We never heard from them again, these people whose eyes pointed to the sun and who had faces of burnished copper.

This is the end of that story.

There is No Word

The Pueblo People have no word that translates as "religion." The knowledge of a spiritual life is a part of the person 2- hours a day, every day of the year. Religious belief permeates every aspect of life. It determines man's relation with the natural world and with his fellow man. The secret of the Pueblo's success was simple. They came face to face with nature but did not exploit it.

Joe S. Sando, Jemez Pueblo
From *Through Indian Eyes*

Some emotions

are forever

impossible to

express with

the arodor

they require.

First Journey

it is dark, dark like the trail
that winds amongst mighty elms,
oaks, and chestnuts at mid of night,
during the black of new moon.
no shape visible except for
the hand holding a buffalo horn,
illuminated by the soft orange glow.

over the embers centered in the Lodge,
the horn tips, water pours forth
upon that single source of light.
Instantly, it is ominous black.
the Lodge is filled with a
searing wet heat that now chokes
the very air desperately required.

the pungent, yet suddenly refreshing
fragrance of sage, fills your lungs
as your Mide Sachem presses a
bundle of the herb to your face.
this is your first Sweat Lodge.
you now are on the good journey
to the end of learned selfness.

you have at last entered the place
where others' needs supplant your own
and the certainty that "they" care
fills the center of your drum.
this part of a complex, refined
and practical religion/medicine that
has protected all the ancestors
from the first parents on, for All of Our
Relations.

a song of the sweat lodge, conceived on
the nineteenth day of the Crackling
Moon, in the four thousand and seventh
season of Little Fog's vision.

> We discard the bonds of reality as surely does the astronaut, when we journey within the Medicine Lodge.

LAKOTA SWEAT LODGE FOR
BLESSED WESTERMAN 1993
MAGNIFIED VALLEY WANN

ARDATH ELK WATERS

Why the Possum's Tail is Bare

Shawnee teaching story

This is an ancient story told by grandparents to the children to teach them of things important. In this telling, I have given it a modern tone for those who have not heard many of the other stories and are, thus, unaware of the great humor that is in the art of storytelling.

In the time before our Grandparents, in the time of the Animal People, there was a great possum. Her name was Grandmother Possum and she was most special. She was an Elder, and the most loved of all the People. But that was not why she was special.

She was smart, and all the young animals would come to her for her sage advice. But that was not why she was special.

Grandmother Possum was special because of her tail. She had a most beautiful, long and bushy tail. Possum was so proud of the silky furred tail that she combed it every day.

Because her tail was so lovely, she would sing her "tail song" whenever the People danced. When they heard her, they would all run to her and ask if they might touch her tail, as it felt so wonderful. Being kind and generous, and well, being a grandmother, she always obliged. She never said no, even when she may be tired or "out of sorts."

All the People agreed, Grandmother Possum's tail was the most beautiful tail in all the Great Turtle Island. This was important because this was the time when there was no light to illuminate her tail. You see, this was in the time before the sun had been found. It was pitch dark, as black as the inside of a rock.

The every day routine was the same. The People would awake and set about their daily jobs. Some would hunt. Others would gather roots and such, and others would just move about as best they could in that darkness.

This was difficult.

There was a lot of, "Umph! Who's there?" as Makwa the Bear, who was the leader of all the People in the Valley of Darkness, would say as he bumped into a soft furry mass.

"It is only me, Wapiti the Elk," would come the reply, "and why did you bumpus, into my rumpus brother bear?"

"Well, mostly because I could not see you," the Bear replied. "You don't even smell like yourself, Wapiti. Did you change your deodorant?" he asked.

The Elk let out a whistle grunt and replied, "Ha, change deodorant? What is deodorant?" he asked.

You see, deodorant had not yet been invented.

"I just was rolling in the new mint that is growing beside the stream, " Elk offered. "Perhaps that is why I don't smell like myself?"

"Perhaps," Bear replied. "Perhaps."

"You know, Wapiti, I am really tired of trying to find my way in this blackness, really tired of bumpus'ing into everyone every day," Bear said sadly.

Now Bear was a great leader, and he put much effort into making the lives of the People in the valley as good as possible. So Bear sat down to think on the problem at hand. He thought and thought for a long time.

Bear suddenly stood up and stated, "I'll ask Creator if we could have some light to see by!" he exclaimed.

The forest suddenly became dead quiet. The birds ceased their chirping and even the wind in the pines went silent. Not a Person made a noise.

"What?" Bear called out. "Now what did I do?"

There was no reply.

"Ok, what's the big joke?" Bear asked.

For a moment it was still silent, then a voice spoke: "You said you were going to-oooot ask Creator why He had not-tttttth given us light-tttttth," Cricket softly replied. "No one ever asked Creator why!"

"Yes!" another voice called out. "W-w-we might l-l-loose all we have if w-w-we ask for more," stammered the rabbit, "No one ever asked Creator why!"

"Well, why not?" the bear asked, now totally confused.

"Perhaps it is because no one has ever thought to before," pondered the old Owl. "Yes indeed, some one should ask!" Owl stated matter-of-factly.

Then the forest became very silent.

"Who would ask?" they all thought to themselves.

A big determined voice sounded out, "Me!" it said. It was Bear again.

"If I was the first to think of it, then I should be the one to ask, it's my job." Bear stated.

The woods were alive with chatter as all the animal People discussed the matter at-hand.

"Yes, Bear should do it," one uttered.

"Only Bear is brave enough," another chimed in.

Yet another of the faceless voices called out, "And he is the only one who is stupid enough."

> Wisdom is given birth from the pain of trying.

"Stop!" Bear yelled. "Stop before I change my mind."

You could hear the breeze whisper in the tree-tops high above, "Bear will asksssssoooooosh!"

And with that Bear raised his head to the black sky and asked, "Oh Great Creator who has given us all, I have a little insignificant question to ask."

Dead silence.

"Well, uhmmm, well, I uhmmm was wondering if you might be able to, well, give us just a tensy ittsy bit of light . . . " he stammered; then in a rush he finished, " . . . so-we-wouldn't-keep-bunpus'ing-into-each-other-all-the-time."

"Whew!" Bear exclaimed, and his voice echoed back and forth through the trees in the valley like leaves being blown by a gust of wind.

Then the forest was even more silent, if that was possible.

A distant rumble began and grew louder. It came crashing throughout the forest making the leaves quiver in the still air. The noise filled all the places where the animal People lived, and they were very frightened.

What had Bear done? What had we done urging him on, they thought.

Through the great noise came a stillness that calmed the valley and its inhabitants.

Then a deep but gentle voice called out, "Bear, what took you so long to ask?"

It was the Voice of Creator.

"Well, sir, I uh, well I . . . " Bear's voice trailed off as he was now afraid of what he had done.

"Bear? Didn't I provide you with a great sense of smell, and keen hearing?" Creator gently asked.

"Yes, oh Great Spirit," Bear said softly, "But . . . "

"But what, my brother?" Creator asked. "Is there a reason why you ask for light?"

Bear was silent. Not that he didn't have an answer but because he was shaking so much, words wouldn't pass his throat. At last he spoke.

"Good Great Mystery, you have given us all we could possibly need, and we are thankful, it is just . . . " Bear paused, ". . . it is just that we are always bumpus'ing into each other, and we thought, well, that is, I thought, with light we wouldn't be bumpus'ing so much that's all."

Again there was a low rumbling that filled the forest and all who had raised their heads to hear, ducked back into their hiding places. The rumbling shook the ground and the trees and the People, too.

Then it changed from a rumble into, well, into a kind of chuckle, then a chortle, and then a big belly laugh. Creator was laughing, and it shook the entire world. No Person could ever remember when Creator had laughed before. This must be a very important time.

Over the roaring laughter and the shaking of the forest and the cries of fear from its inhabitants, a voice could be heard. It was Bear.

"Oh, Great Spirit, I am most honored that I could make you laugh, but are you happy or angry?"

The laughter slowed to a snicker and then Creator was silent.

"Bear, it has been a very long time since I have been so pleased," Creator spoke. "I gave you wisdom and you resolved a problem. I gave you courage and you came to me. I gave you a voice and you have asked me for a favor. But most important, I gave you free will to choose, and you chose to come to me to help with your problem." Creator paused.

"My dear brother bear, you please me," the Spirit stated. "Now what was it that you asked for . . . ? Oh yes, light. So be it."

Now Creator spoke to all the People. "If one of you can go to the Great Cave where the heat of summer blows forth, and you go deep into the cave, you will find two glowing embers by a great fire. Take the embers from their place beside the fire and bring them out of the cave and into the forest," he stated. "Then I will give you light."

"Yes, but . . . " started Bear. But the air was now still and the aura of Creator's presence was no longer in the forest. "But . . . I was just going to ask who should go for the embers," Bear said dejectedly.

In unison, the many voices of the forest called out, "You silly. You asked; you got the job."

This made sense to Bear, and he started off towards the Great Cave of the summer heat. It was a short journey as the valley was small. Soon he was at the entrance. Turning back to his fellow forest People he said, "Well, here I go! But if I don't come out soon, please feel free to come find me."

With that, he entered the cave. Soon they could no longer hear the sounds of his giant claws as they clicked on the cave floor. Bear was now deep into the cave.

As Bear felt his way along the wall of the winding cave, he soon felt a new experience. His fur was warmer, but he was aware that his eyes were trying to focus on something. This was unique since his eyes had been of no use in the black dark of the forest. Indeed, bear was experiencing a new sensation, sight.

As he rounded a curve in the dim glow of the cave, he was able to see a few stones alongside the path. In fact, he could see the path. This newfound sensation of sight hurt his eyes as he was not yet accustomed to it.

Soon he was eagerly exploring the cave with his eyes. The light became brighter and brighter and then as he came around yet another bend in the cave, he stepped out before a great fire.

Its flames flickered in the darkness of the cave casting wonderfully scary shadows all about. Bear was very excited over all this, and he let out a big roar.

"Roooooarrrrr!" he exclaimed and it echoed all through the cave, startling him as it cascaded down the path and out the Great Cave entrance.

"Oh my! Bear is hurt," Crow offered.

"Or afraid," snickered Snake. (Snake was always bad-mouthing the other People.)

"Hush up, Snake, before I sit on you," Badger shouted.

The bear was anxious to see more as the fire was most mysterious and entrancing; but remembering his mission, he edged closer to the fire. At first, it felt warm like it was when he, as a cub had slept with his mother in the den. But as he drew closer, he got hotter. It was so hot that he had to pant for relief.

At last he was close enough to the coals by the edge of the great fire to touch them. As he gingerly stretched out his arm to take an ember and leave, the heat became so intense that it charred the bottom of his paw black.

"EEEyooooo!" he cried out in pain. "That hurt!"

He tried again with each paw, with the same painful results. Injured and in pain, he made his way back into the darkness and into the valley of his ancestors.

When the bear returned, the People all smelled his singed hair and burnt paws and asked, "What happened?"

Bear told them of the bright light and the painful heat, and of the burns he had incurred.

"I am a failure," he told his companions. "You had expected me to bring light but all I bring is my failure and shame." He lowered his head and sat near a big bolder beside the cave to tend to his injuries.

Badger stepped towards the cave and announced, "Bear did not fail. His claws were just not long enough. I have the longest, and toughest claws in the valley. I can get the ember," he stated with great confidence.

Into the cave he went.

Out of the cave he came . . . with no ember.

Same story: The embers were too hot to hold.

Animal after animal went into the cave and came back without an ember.

The People were becoming sad . . . and disappointed. The promise of light was slipping away as each of them came back without an ember.

Now Grandmother Possum had been sitting nearby doing what Grandmother Possum always did, preening her beautiful fur and singing her song softly.

But Possum was listening intently.

After the last brave soul had attempted to retrieve an ember, and had failed, Grandmother Possum at last stopped preening and stepped towards the cave entrance.

"I have been thinking," she said.

"And . . . ?" all the People said in unison.

"I have heard that each of our brave friends have failed because they could not hold an ember long enough to bring it out of the cave, right?" she stated.

"Yes, that is truth," they all replied.

"I think that the fur on my tail is so thick that I would not get burnt carrying the ember from the cave," she offered. "If I can just get the ember onto my tail, I will succeed," she said with great confidence.

"Oh my, that is a great idea," Weasel said as he was licking his burned fingers.

"Yes indeed," said Bear. And the rest of the People agreed.

"Be careful, Grandmother Possum," they all said as she entered the cave.

Like the others who had traveled the cave's path before her, she too had to become accustomed to the light and the heat. Soon she was at the Great Fire.

"Mmmm," she pondered, "it is indeed very hot."

Looking about the fire's edge, she spotted a single ember that had fallen to the ground and had rolled a short distance from the blaze.

Edging closer to the intense heat, she reached out to grab the hot ember in her paw to toss it into her tail fur.

"Ouch!" she cried out in pain as the heat burned the hair from her paw, and making her fingers hurt. The beautiful fur on her hands had been singed black-gray, as was much of her fur elsewhere. Only her beautiful tail was still intact.

"This is going to be harder than I thought," she said as she sat down to ponder the situation. With determination that only a grand-mother can possess, Possum thought of different plans.

At last she was ready.

"If I can run quickly up to the fire and scoop an ember, I can toss it into my tail fur and run it down the cave to the valley and send it skyward to Creator," she said, "If I can do all this very fast, I may not get burnt too badly."

So, just as she had planned, Grandmother Possum ran up to the fire and with her nose, she flipped the ember into her tail and ran quickly back to the valley. This burnt her nose but she was determined to bring light to her People. And she knew that she could not fail Creator.

At the entrance of the cave, she spun around and launched the still red ember into the sky.

Instantly, Creator took it and made it into the sun. In that same instant, there was now light.

Everyone cheered and pointed to the bright light in the sky, exclaiming their joy. At last there was light in the valley. Now they could see everything . . . just as soon as their eyes adjusted to this new experience of light.

The forest was filled with light, and the chattering of the valley inhabitants.

Looking about, they were able to see the magnificent trees and the grand mountains and the sweet water that flowed in the stream in the center of the valley. At last they could see how each person looked.

"Hey, everybody, Raccoon has stripes!" said Badger with glee, "and the Cardinal Bird is red!"

"There is Bear," Rabbit exclaimed. "See, his paws are black from the time he burned them in the cave." The chatter rolled across the valley as each person spoke of their being able to see all things. There was great joy in the valley.

Then Bear rose and held up his hand to quiet the People. He wanted to speak. "I for one am most thankful that Creator has given us light," he said. Continuing, "To you, oh Great Creator, we give our thanks and love," he said in prayer.

"Ayeia," sang out the others in agreement and praise.

"And to Grandmother for her bravery and determination, we now have our sun," Bear continued. Then he looked around to find her. But Grandmother Possum was not to be seen.

The People called out for her, but she did not answer. They began to look for their hero who had given them light. They looked in the trees and under the bushes. They looked to the mountain and the stream but they could not find her. At last, Chipmunk looked behind the great rock at the entrance of the cave and found her. She was hiding.

"Grandmother Possum," Bear called out, "are you alright?"

"Yes, I am, but please leave me alone," she replied. "I am no longer beautiful. I am ugly." she said softly and began to cry.

As the People looked upon her they saw that the beautiful fur on her hands and face had been burned away, leaving her mottled with singed fur and bare hands and nose. But the most disturbing sight was her tail. In carrying the ember down the cave and into the valley, she had burned off every strand of the lovely fur from her tail. Her tail was now bare to the pink flesh.

Grandmother Possum was mortified. The person that all the People had called the most beautiful of the valley was now a singed and bare, ugly animal. She was so ashamed that she lowered herself even closer to the ground and tried to scrunch herself under a giant stone.

Then she heard a great sound.

Everyone was cheering. They were shouting her name over and over and calling her to come out to receive the respect due her. They continued until she obliged. The valley was filled with sound as the People all expressed their thanks and love for this most grand and brave person.

At last she came out to thank them. She was still ashamed of her appearance but was most gracious as she thanked them for their praise and love.

Then the valley began to rumble again. The wind blew hard and the light became intense at the entrance of the cave. A great voice boomed out.

"Our beloved Grandmother Possum has given that which she felt was her most valued asset; her long fur. It is gone forever, and she feels that she is no longer worthy of being in your midst," Creator's voice echoed across the valley. "But we all love her and we all wish to honor her," Creator continued. "How may we do this and yet honor her wishes not to be seen?"

The valley was now very quiet as all thought of a solution to their dilemma.

Then Creator spoke again. "Why did I not think of this sooner? I will make Grandmother Possum a place to live where she can still be with the People of the valley and yet not be seen. I will divide the light in two and make half the time dark, as it was before she gave us the ember," Creator stated with great satisfaction. "I will call the light time day and the dark time night."

"That is all grand and wonderful, Creator," Bear timidly asked, " I don't want to seem a nitpick, but won't we will still be bumpus'ing into the rumpus in the night?"

With that, Creator turned to Grandmother Hummingbird. "Sister Hummingbird, will you fly to the top of the sky and use your long slender beak to punch many holes into the sky?"

Quick as a wink, she flew high and darting back and forth she made a fine pattern of holes in the roof of the valley. Then she retired to rest from her work.

"Thank you, Grandmother Hummingbird," Creator exclaimed. "That was just what I had envisioned. As the light of day slowly dims for night, my light will still shine through the holes in the sky."

Creator paused and then stated, "I will call the tiny light that brightens the night sky stars."

"And now I know how we can honor Grandmother Possum," Creator said. "I will make her the Great Leader of the night and Bear the Great Leader of the day!"

It was said. It was done.

So it was that the People of the valley had bright light in the day and tiny lights at night, and they never had to go bumpus'ing into each other again.

Bear was a good leader of the day making sure that all the questions of the People had a good answer and that all the People were healthy and happy.

And Grandmother Possum was most pleased to be the leader of the night, where she could be with the People and yet not have them feel sorry for her looks mostly because they could not see her very well. In time, she developed great night vision and did rule the night in a good and proper manner.

So, if you see a possum, you will always remember that it was Possum's great sacrifice for the People that gave us light and the night with the stars. And you will remember why she looks as she does and know that she is the Great Leader of the night.

That is the end of this story.

3   Of the Soul and Spirituality

Our religion is not one of paint and feathers. It is a
thing of the heart.

Follower of Handsome Lake, Seneca
From *Through Indian Eyes*

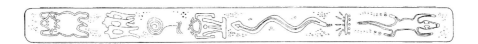

Red Fox Camp

morning smoke lay near grass
as red orange of first light
filters through trees into
the place of sacred blue water.
muffled cough, soft sleep sounds
gently emanate from lodge walls
as elders sit in last/first council.
wings silent float in final hunt
above the meadow for four-footed
ventured foolishly to search for grain.
life continued, life at end –
the circle of time passes without
pause for all quiet, all aware.
it is the nature of being.
the rhythm is constant beating,
the drum in the heart of Creation
repeats endlessly without pause.
we sleep, wake, sadness, joy,
to sound eternal, dream, vision
pain, delight in this circle
stretched atop the bowl of spirits.
morning smoke rises black night,

frees color, sweet effusive in
power tangible, infinite.
first smoke rises to carry
in sacred cloud, prayers for
those yet in slumber, meditation,
or on their seventh journey.
the circle is unbroken.

A song at the coming of first light as we celebrate the year of the indigenous people. Conceived on the ninth day of the red paint moon, in the four thousand and eighth season of Little Fog's Vision.

Sunrise begins,

sunset ends . . .

to that we have

no control

except for what

is between.

BREAD DANCE VILLAGE
SHAWNEE. JRB
BROWN EAGLE LAKE
URBANA, OHIO

Walk in Balance

One of my favorite statements is to "Walk in Balance." Most who hear it for the first time are either puzzled as to its meaning or immediately adopt it for their own. Yet few have a grasp of the concept of "Walk in Balance" as it is understood by the Shawnee. We are told that Balance is a state of being connected with all things, that everything we do has a profound effect on everything else in all Creation.

In our oral tradition, we learn that Walking in Balance is more akin to being placed at birth on an ancient, house-sized slab of rough gray stone. The somewhat flat surface is cracked and worn in a timeless manner with tuffs of grass and plants emerging from the cracks in some places. As you live your life, everything has an impact on your stone's balance. If a butterfly or a rain drop lands on your stone, you have to adjust your position to accommodate that change in balance. You must do this in a graceful manner as not to cause your stone to wobble. If a bolder or a mob of two-leggeds jump onto your stone, your job is the same keep your stone in balance. All this must be done in an agile way, being ever nimble.

On the bottom of this stone, slightly off-center, is a small singular point of stone carefully steadied on a stone below it. That is the stone of your parents, and it is balanced on their parents' stone, and so it is back to the First Parents.

When you have children, their stone will be balanced on yours, and their children's children into the future. The whole tower is balanced upon the foundation of Creation.

> **Think!**
>
> It's our job.

Each move you make, each thought, each action can cause the entire stack to wobble or shake. It is your job to keep it all in balance throughout your life. Now all this makes one think about their own lives and how all others are dependent on your ability to keep in balance.

All this is called the Walk of Life, or the Dance of Life.

So the next time someone says, "Stay in balance," or you hear me say, "Walk in Balance," you will know that they really mean to live your life in a manner in which you will cause as little harm and discomfort to others as possible, being ever mindful that your every action will cause a change in the world forever to the good, or the bad.

May we always Walk in Balance.

The Place

The Day the Sioux Ran

In 1984, the Medicine Wheel Feather Flag of the Tribal Chairman's Association of the many Indian Nations was carried by Sioux runners from New York to Los Angeles. This was to honor the occasion of the United States hosting the 1984 Summer Olympics, and to deliver the message from the Chairmen to the International Olympic Committee at the Summer Olympics, held in Los Angeles that summer.

Indeed the Great Spirit was with us that day as we prepared to receive the band of our brothers, the Sioux.. These runners were brave men, young and old who took turns carrying the Sacred Feather Flag across the Great Turtle Island.

The staff had been created expressly for this occasion by the Elders of their Nation. For nearly a moon circle, they took turns carrying the flag. They were carrying the Sacred Message entrusted to them by the great leaders of the many nations of Native Americans. Americans— a word that has come to fill the hearts and souls of so many with pride. Still, it has a lingering taste of pecan hulls to those whose thoughts and Spirit are of the Ancient Ones. Yet, we are proudly American Patriots, first and always.

The run began at the edge of the waters where the sun rises in New York City. Each day they shared the honor of carrying the staff between the members of this chosen group, and with the many Native Americans and friends they encountered along the way. In all weather, day after day, they proceeded with dedication that they would reach their destination at the steps of the Coliseum—where the 1984

Summer Olympic Games were to be held—and to take their place in the Opening ceremonies.

As the first glint of the new day warmed the horizon, a great Council of many nations assembled. There were Navaho, Apache, Azteca, Zuni, and men and women from the Great Plains. People from the Mountains of the West and of the Woodlands and Lakes (where the runners had first started) had gathered.

> Our good works are ended only if we stop.

The sun burned hot early, as it was the season of first harvest. Special care had been taken to sweep the camp clean and to prepare a great quantity of food and gifts for our guests. The people had come together, near the eve of the night of the Hawk and the Owl, to hold Council and make ready a celebration for this most historic event. Then we danced and sang of other glorious days, long past, well into the indigo blue of late night. Now all thoughts centered on the moment that was soon to be.

In our presence were many noble people, including the family of the great Jim Thorpe and government officials represented the great nations of the United States and Canada. There were many brothers and sisters, fine artisans who had given of their skills to show others how we truly live and think.

We were inspired and guided by the leadership and the spirit of the great Cherokee Indian Iron Eyes Cody and the Oglala Lakota, Yellowhair. Our village chief was an Iroquois, Lyman Pierce, of the Southern California Indian Centers.

All those present were joined by many non-Indians, including the important people who had been chosen to deliver the long-traveled message from the American Indian Leaders that these braves had carried across the Great Turtle Island.

Drums and hearts beat-as-one, and the voice of the People sang in joy, as the word was passed, "They are near."

We pressed to the edge of camp to get a first glimpse of our brothers as they rounded into sight. Many young men and women ran out to meet the tired band and accompanied them as they entered the Council arena.

Our proud and joyful hearts filled to near bursting as we saw the Medicine Totem carried by the first runner. Its feathers seemed to lift the Sacred Hoop higher, as the runners and crowd pressed into the camp.

Chants and cries filled the air, and many drums told of the great victory this day. The message from the Tribal Chairman's Association was read to the people gathered in our temporary village, and all could see the brave men who had carried this Totem.

Grouped with the original band were young men from many nations who had joined them along the way. Even a boy of eleven or twelve had run many days. At times, when the older men were tired, he would take the lead and inspire the others on. The pipe was lit and food and drink were given. Afterwards, when the excitement had subsided, and gifts were exchanged . . . the stories of their many encounters were told and retold.

That same day, the message of the Council of Nations was given to the Great Chief of the Village of Los Angeles . . . Mayor Bradley, and to the rest of the world. It was received by leaders at the Olympic gathering of the many Nations, at the summer games that early harvest season. It is sad to note that the message that had been so openly carried across the United States was not (as had been promised), read during the Opening Ceremonies, but, rather, was received in private the following day by a representative of the Olympic Committee.

It was the shame of the organizers that this important welcoming message from the First People of the Great Turtle Island had not been delivered to the world as the Olympic people had promised. The Sioux had kept their word. They had delivered the message.

The story of the strength and bravery of these Sioux runners who had carried the message of peace and love from our People to the rest of the world, will long endure.

I Have Seen the Promise
So Often Broken, Made Whole

It is told to us by the Ancestors, in our oral traditions, that when we need to seek knowledge to see the important things we must go on a quest, a spiritual search, and to walk on the other side of the Veil of this life. This long held tradition has revealed our greatest guidance and wisdom. I, like my grandparents before me, have made this prayer-walk to ask for understanding. For I am a two-legged, and am in want, to find the true way, the good road for All My Relations.

I have heard their drum and I have had a mighty vision. I have seen a great nation of my People united in a common cause across the breadth of the Turtle Island. I have heard the voice of the People sing out in unity, rejoicing in the realization that once again we are a strength to be reckoned.

I have seen a vision where the Red Nation of many sticks are considered equal with all others and where our voice is a part of all that causes this grand country to work. I have seen a vision of the return of our sovereignty and the making of a treaty that can never be broken.

Tecumseh, the great leader of the Shawnee in the last days of the freedom of his people said, "The way, and the only way to end this wrong, is for all the Red People to unite, in claiming a common and equal right in the land as it was at first, and yet should be."

I have seen the promise so often broken, made whole. Not in a cloud or in the smoke of a prayer-pipe, but in the crystal clear air of truth. I have seen the birth of the Red Peoples emancipation, the sovereign Red Nation, the fifty first state of this great United States of America.

A state non-contiguous, each county being the existing place of the individual Treated Nations, with additional federal land to be provided that all Native American Tribes and Bands will have a place to call their own. Each Nation, a county with representation in the state legislator; this new state co-equal, with appropriate seats in the Senate and House where at last we will have the long promised representation in the mother government, the United States Congress. No longer will we have to be the step-child of the host state where within its boundaries our greatness lay.

Simply put, a new state, a fifty-first star on the Stars and Stripes, where each tribe is a county and each native person has one vote. We can be a state that will return the green grass and the blue waters that have so long been denied by our being part-time citizens. A state where we will at last be true, full Americans.

There need not be loss to any particular existing state as tribal lands are not part of a state, but federal held lands. This new star on the flag will shine as a dignified end to the 500 years of shameful and immoral attempts to destroy our culture, our sacred places, and has been the cause of the unnecessary deaths of thousands upon thousands of the original People of this Turtle Island.

With Honor and respect restored, our great American nation can begin to heal this wound.

For, if a society, no matter how strong, cannot resolve the wrongs caused by it's creation, it can never possess real honor or integrity. Despite proclamations and protestations, a nation bereft of these most basic qualities can not prevail as a truly free society.

Without this, we the People, all the people of this United States, are doomed to die from our inherited shame. The continued eradication of the way and life of the first people will ultimately destroy us all.

I have had a vision where all People, of all diversities, in this great nation, are united equally in honor and dignity. Then we will be allowed to set the example for all the world. Until that time I pray that we will strive to that goal . . . together.

A great statesman of the Six Nations Confederacy of the Iroquois who held the ancient title Tododaho, Leon Shenadoah said, "These are our times and our responsibilities. Every human being has a sacred duty to protect the welfare of our mother earth, from whom all life comes (and her children). In order to do this we must recognize the enemy, the one within us. We must begin with ourselves."

The Gift of New Life

Know that each day is the gift of new life. Each day you are born again into the light after the death passage of sleep. You should welcome this gift of a new day with song. Sometimes I sing this one . . .

The rock that was placed on my head when I went to sleep and that has held me dead, becomes the sun in the place that life begins. Once again, He who creates with His Mind has given me this life to live today.

Let me just once this day speak of good things, show a sheltered path to those I meet. Help me use my power of the touch to make this day a better one for someone. Then when the death of night once again returns, I will be worthy of another gift of life.

May I live this song. Sing this song to the Sky People, to the Earth People, and to all the People of Creation.

This is my prayer, this is my song, oh, Kiji Manito.

Live this song.

Sing it to the Sky People, to the Earth People and to all the People of Creator.

4   Markers in the Forests

And when your children's children think themselves
alone in the field . . . or in the silence of the pathless
woods, they will not be alone.

Attributed to Chief Seattle, 1855
From *Through Indian Eyes*

Creation and Growing Up Indian

Thoughts and comments by Tom Hill (Seneca), Richard Hill, Jr. (Tuscarora), and Jim Great Elk Waters (Shawnee) . . .

There is a magic of childhood within the Indian-way that is so absent in the outside world today.

The native understanding of the world begins with the Creation. The many elaborate Creation stories are the best means to understand our world views. Original stories teach us what kind of people we hope to become, what kind of contribution we hope to make, what kind of legacy we hope to pass on to our children. In some ways, life's journey is an effort to keep the wisdom from the time of Creation a part of our everyday existence.

Iroquoians, like many other natives, believe that the Creation is ongoing and that people were placed on earth to re-create the Creator's good works—that is, to be creators.

Children are born within circles of tradition that define the world views of their communities. For example, an Iroquoian child's first moccasins are punctured to keep the relationship between the child and the earth intact.

Each culture has a distinctive philosophy about how to raise children. In the past, many native groups used cradleboards. Strapped in the vertical cradles, children saw the world from the same viewpoint as adults. Today they still are

> We hold the code to the magic of yesterdays as long as we recall our youth, and we can visit when we desire if we but recall.

surrounded by symbolism that is their first introduction to the world they have entered. Each symbol is a token of the stories and traditions that they will be told repeatedly, to learn as they grow up.

Children learn by observing. They learn through the rhythms of the community, the songs, dances, and annual cycles of rituals and events. The Jewish writer/philosopher Dennis Prager laments "the absence of ritual today." He notes that this absence "has removed many of the necessary markers of life."

There was, traditionally, a seasonal calendar for storytelling, setting a rhythm of learning. Through stories, the ways of the ancestors were made real for children, and the world around them became a powerful place.

Learning to tell stories starts with learning to listen. To show respect for storytellers and other speakers, children were taught not to interrupt. Ogallala-Lakota elder Standing Bear wrote, "to look when there was apparently nothing to see, and listen intently when all seemingly was quiet."

Try to imagine what it was like to grow up in a time when making things was a never-ending part of daily life. Household goods, hunting equipment, clothing, and religious objects were produced within the community. Every day included artistic creation and spiritual expression. Children were surrounded by artists.

Think of what childhood must have been like for the child who wore a colorful shirt his mother had made, so much like his father's shirt. Or the children who watched their father carve his bow drill, knowing he was sharing with them his happiness in his life, in his work, and love of the world.

These worlds of creativity and imagination still exist. Many native households today make traditional clothing for powwows and ceremonies, utensils for rituals, objects of spiritual faith, and power. Today, as in the past, nearly every native person is related to an artist. The creative process is still an integral part of growing up. It's our job.

Ohio-Seppe

Cool sand mud wets my flesh
as I rest engrossed at water's edge
watching this brown wet ribbon
flow through the tree-lined banks
of the giver of life, Ohio-seppe.

Toes burrowed beneath
tobacco tint silt lain here
in rhythm endless since glacier-melt
first trickled along new-sprung,
now ancient water pathways.

Bone-frames of trees and brush
erosion felled along the margin
of this enchanted water's flow as it
courses through the spectacle
of grove and field, branch and brook.

Oh, how I love this place of solitude
where the spirits of other places
and other folk roll beneath my feet
being part of the whole that is here
Not two-legged but of mud-water.

Returned to the root of life given
the blood of the land includes me
in its wandering rush to other places
in need also of its healing powers
oblivious to all, vigilant always.

Man now, first child always drawn
Moth like here for a century half
In sheer wonderment of its reality
this ever-changing gathered rain
And well and spring flow endless,

Recalled catlike or monster fish
Caught, or washed ashore found,
all their descendants apparitions,
in reality alive within the
now green satin mirror surface.

Change is rule to this water Gift
that enchants me so with its Voice
and scent and air that fills the
valley floor it claims home
for long millennium to now.

Oh, sing your songs to once more
as in truth and memory entwined

of the warrior, woman, and child with
toy upon the skin of this vessel
songs of past, and yet to come.

Sing to me of grandness, of steam
and wheeled riverman's home
floating to destination and port chosen
of their chanteys and spirits and mirth
of the naive joy abandoned upon you.

And tell once again of the sad horror
of lived rains and snows too profuse
causing you to grow and engulf
home and field and life as you continue
your journey west then south to sea.

Of the spring water-fed lush greens
of autumns filled color who defy equal
of snow softened blankets that edged
and summer fires life-quenched
at your impartial bluff and shore.

of stories told again to ears new
share with me for i am yet child
in time worn skin age wrinkled by the
yellow red sky-fire that has tried to
exhaust your moist soul for all time.

And yet to the sun and cloud and wind
to each in its need you have shared
your abundance cycle without passion or care
as known purpose or thoughtless venture
continue to drink from your sweet excess.

Without care or cause I lay beside you
once more to infuse my spirit with your
gift and to fill my memories once again
of reason and dream, of smiles and woe
fulfilling my connectedness to life anew.

Lives lived full

demands we

spent time

in place, to

observe that

which we would

otherwise have

never beheld.

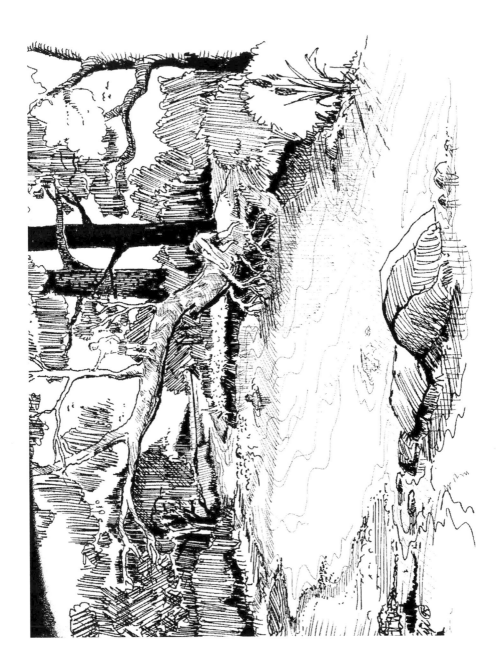

The Shawnee Woman

She walks the red road
of tradition, of blood,
gentle with children,
gifted extreme patience.

Uncommon strength imbued
and genuine nature always,
a leader by instinct
thinks forever Southwind.

Knowledge of skills, survival
personify with mate-tribe
female eternally, feminine,
contemplative, and compassionate.

She is the never ceasing,
great counterbalance Gift
to all, from the first musings
to Veil if this life-fading.

On Character

It is said that, "The measure of one's character is not what we get from our ancestors, but what we leave our descendants." This is our character. Here are a few thoughts to ponder on the subject.

Character Traits: Each of us has three character traits: that which we exhibit—what others perceive; that we think we have—our ego; and that which we are. Get to know each well and keep them in their rank of importance.

Cultivate Your Character: Our character is like the evergreen tree. All its capability for being a beautiful mature tree is developed in its first years. But without nourishment and warmth, even the hardiest evergreen will wither and die. Like the evergreen, we need to care for and build upon the character we developed in our youth.

Weed Our Garden: We need to pay close attention to those distractions that will rob us of our core values. We must be ever wary of compromise in what we feel most important.

Laughter: Or, more importantly, what excites you to laugh is a sign of developing character or a declining integrity.

Beware of Erosion: We often do not notice what qualities we are losing until they are almost gone.

Reinforce You Value System: Like a fence, all the whitewash applied will never strengthen your nature.

Once you know what you have, forget it. Character works best in that environment. Know what you stand for, won't stand for. Others will evaluate your character by the height of your principles, the breadth of your compassion, the depth of your conviction, and the length of your patience.

Character speaks loudest with action.

Having good character is not enough. You will never be what you ought to be until you are doing what you ought to be doing.

The practice of your principles will be the passing on of the gifts you received as your tree grew strong and tall.

Find time to shelter the weak; assist them as you would a relative, for they are. It is said by the Lakota that "All things are connected."

Be a landmark to those wandering. Offer to be a mentor to someone in your fields. Help them develop the traits that have made you the "who" that you are.

Remember, no person is better than their principles.

It Is Now

a smell of sweet grass and
sage is infinite, unending.
close mother kind warmth
of the moist lodge flows
as this special time,
obeys a most sacred and
parallel nature.

the flame in the center fire
does ritual dance on the wall
and spirit relics, important gifts
that surround the two as they
ready this age for new life.
blankets of skin, wraps of fur
are near for their use yet here.

sucking breath, hot windblown
creation comes quickly and
the water flows from the spring
of all life two-legged.
it is now, it is time for the
work of Creator's child grown as
the cords' new sound is issued.

The Good Great Spirit who
creates with Its thought
has envisioned anew, that
which the Manitou incepted

when the first She was begot.
again the circle is completed.
again she has caused morrow.
The cord is unbroken.

A song of the birthing lodge as we celebrate the year of the indigenous people. Conceived on the ninth day of the Red Paint Moon, in the one thousand and eighth season of Little Fog's Vision.

The Sacred Weed

From *Through Indian Eyes* with comments by Jim Great Elk Waters.

In recent times, we have been bombarded with news on tobacco. There has been a lot of data, proven and suspect, about this plant. However, few know how the Indian views this sacred herb. This is not about the reports available but to, as Paul Harvey would say, " . . . the rest of the story."

Tobacco: Almost no ceremony could take place without it. Every tribal council, each call to arms or move towards peace was prefaced by smoking it. Cherokee medicine men squeezed its juice on bee stings and snakebites and boiled its leaves into a tea as a cure for fever. The Creek crumbled it into the postholes of new houses, believing it would drive away ghosts. Such were the virtues of tobacco, a substance of countless uses and deep mystical importance.

Indians used tobacco to clear the mind, calm the soul, stave off hunger, and for sheer enjoyment. Its principal virtues, however, were spiritual. Just as the flame of the Council fire was thought to be a piece of the sun transported to the earth, so the smoke from the burning tobacco was seen as a prayer rising up to the Great Spirit. Before the high priests lit the New Year's fire in the Green Corn Ceremony, leaves of tobacco were placed in the fire pit. Tribal members smoked tobacco to ward off evil, cast out witches, heal the sick, bring rain, and ensure fair

> We so fear the potential that we fill our thoughts with lies to make our position credible.

weather before a journey. So potent were its effects, in fact, that when someone rose in Council with a pipe in his hand, his listeners knew he would speak only the truth. And whenever two foes sat down to parley, the smoke of the peace pipe would cleanse their hearts and ensure that their accord would last forever.

It was not until after the Europeans and the rest of the world took up tobacco consumption that the problems associated with it developed. Perhaps if they had held tobacco as sacred as the Red Man, we would not have this problem today.

5   Of Indians Today

I can tell you there are no secrets. There's no mystery.
There is only common sense.

Oren Lyons, The Onondaga Tadodaho
From *Through Indian Eyes*

Poverty of the Mind

It is a disgrace that shames Our Ancestors.

I am filled to the gullet with the "pity parties" and diatribes against the United States from which some Indian People seem to get gratification. They are quick to blame our government for the "plight" of the American Indian. They lay the full blame of Indian poverty on the United States and its lack of administrative responsibilities. There is some truth in their claims, but much of the blame is ours. We Indians have accepted poverty as a way of life. We have come to embrace that thoughtless lie as a fact and live in impoverished conditions as if to say we believe this claptrap.

Being without is a serious matter. No American should have to live in poverty. Those are things we must address and end, but poverty of the mind is a disgrace that also shames our ancestors. Most of our Native American families have known hardship and poverty, but there are a great many families who have not allowed themselves to wallow in that condition.

Hell, I was raised in rural Appalachia and experienced firsthand the syndrome that can entice one to accept poverty as their lifestyle. And I have seen that there is no reason that a person would have to long-endure such conditions. It is a problem that can be solved. To say otherwise is to lie to oneself.

It makes me sad in my Center Place to think on the plight of our People who won't, for whatever the reason, end the cycle of destruction and make

> Ignorance and sloth fulfill the prophecy of regret.

a good place of where they sit. Our Ancestors were ever improving and adapting to make their lives better.

I can't recall any Oral Histories that dwell on being a loser. To the contrary, they are stories of great accomplishments and personal character motivation.

Yes, there are still a lot of things to be righted; and with diligent effort and positive attitudes, they will, in time, be corrected.

We, as the Children of the Earth, have always been challenged. As it was in the time of our Grandparents, it is our responsibility to walk the Red-Road in a good way and become the best two-leggeds possible.

It is not our birthright to live the wrong-minded role of the victim. I am filled with compassion and heartfelt pain, but do not accept that this is the fate they must endure.

As Tecumseh said, "We are the makers of our destiny."

For me, being Indian is a Blessing and an uplifting experience. It causes me to hold myself proud and gives me the Balance that makes me who I am. I am honored and so very proud that Creator thought to cause part of my Ancestors to be Turtle Island First People.

I choose not to be a statistic on poverty. I choose to do as my Ancestors did, to cause myself to be the "maker of my destiny."

We are the Ones

Listen closely, I will not repeat this today.
I bring you a Blessing,
a Message,
and a Destination.
Take notes if you wish.

The Blessing of No

I asked Creator to remove my feelings of self-importance.
Creator said, "No."
"It is not for me to remove this feeling you dislike.
It is your job to make it go away."

I asked Creator to grant me tolerance.
Creator said, "No."
"Tolerance wells up from disrespect.
Tolerance isn't granted, it is earned."

I asked Creator to fill me with cheer.
Creator again said, "No."
"I give you Blessings, finding that which brings you cheer, is up to you."

I asked Creator to free me from anguish.
Creator said, "No."

"Anguish draws you apart from worldly pleasures and
brings you closer to me."

I asked Creator to make my Spirit grow.
Creator said, "No."
"You must grow on your own, but I will trim you to
make you fruitful."

I asked for all things that might allow me to more
enjoy life.
Creator said, "No."
"I will give you life so that you may enjoy all things."

I asked Creator to teach me to love others, as He
loves me.
Creator said, "Ahhhh, finally you understand!"

The leaf's singular existence is to live for the time it makes it's journey earthward to nourish it's seed.

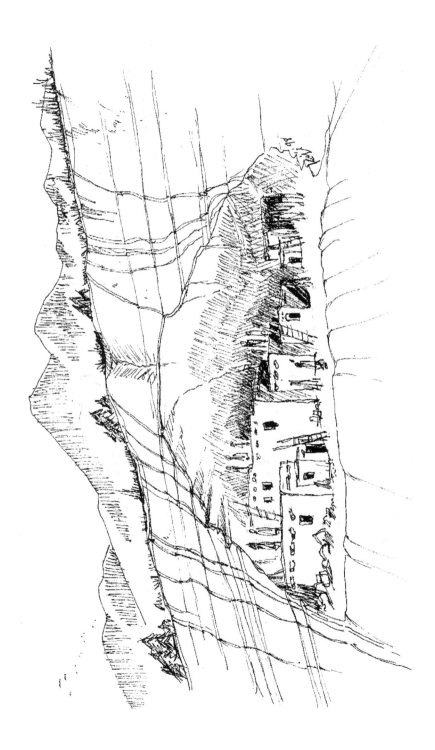

A Message

An anonymous Hopi Prophet from the Third Mesa, Old Oraibi, Arizona.

Grandfather asked me to send to you the following words . . . "You have been telling the People that this is the Eleventh Hour, now you must go back and tell the People that this is the Hour . . . and there are things to be considered . . .

"Where are you living?

"What are you doing?

"What are your relationships?

"Are you in the right relationship?

"Where is your water?

"Know your garden.

"It is time to speak your Truth.

"Create your community.

"Be good to each other.

"And do not look outside yourself for the leader."

Then he clasped his hands together, smiled, and said, "This could be a good time!"

"There is a river flowing now very fast. It is so great and swift that there are those who will be afraid. They will try to hold on to the shore.

They will feel they are being torn apart and will suffer greatly. Know the river has its destination. The elders say we must let go of the shore, push off into the middle of the river, keep our eyes open and our heads above the water. And I say, see who is in there with you and celebrate."

"At this time in history, we are to take nothing personally, least of all, ourselves, for the moment that we do, our spiritual growth and journey comes to a halt. The time of the lone wolf is over. Gather yourselves! Banish the word "struggle" from your attitude and your vocabulary. All that we do now must be done in a sacred manner and in celebration."

Again he fell silent for a while. Then he added: Tell them: "WE ARE THE ONES WE'VE BEEN WAITING FOR!"

Oraibi, Hopi Nation

The Destination

It is told by the Elders of my Mide'wiian-Coashellaqua faith that we are the center of our universe, that we are the source of all that which is about us, that we have absolute control of our path, our destiny.

We hold this to be a truth.

If we are therefore the center of our universe, then it is our job, our responsibility, to make our journey to our Destination Not Yet Known one of clarity and honor. We must understand the lessons of the past but must not let that knowledge control the path before us.

It is not the mistakes and learnings of our past human journeys but the Light, the Source from which we Origin'ed that is the Spirit Guide to that Destination.

Make not this mistake once again, the mistake that has caused us distrust and hate and to lose our path to the sought after peace for which we all so yearn.

As long we relive the mistakes of the past, we will never be able to embrace a future in peace.

It is that simple.

It is a consummate truth that for as long as we live the past distrust and hate, we will never be able to experience the truth of love . . .

that wellspring of peace.

You have heard the Prayer of No . . .

You have heard the wisdom of the Hopi Prophet.

 "We are the ones."

You now know the Destination . . .

The choice is, as it has always been, YOURS!

In the Rain

From an article submitted by MaxBluWing in the back pages of Chautauqu—Echoes in the Wind, *June 1, 1997. Author unknown.*

The gentle rain speaks upon the soft earth and God is in the midst of the mist reminding us that the brightness of sunshine is on the other side of every dark cloud. Droplets dance in silence as they are introduced to the world. We have been here before they say and are here again to refresh

> **We are made in God's Image, not the obverse.**

and bless. As the moon reflects the light of the sun, nature reflects the beauty of God.

I am not angry with the world but with its two-legged dwellers. Dwellers who want to look through a tube at stars they can't already see or investigate biomes of invisible nature. Dwellers that can't hear the rain sing to the Creator the appreciation of just being or hear a child say I love you. Dwellers that can't answer the birds when they tell you not to worry, everything will be OK, or just enjoy being one of the People thankful for the corn of today. The soft rain whispers.

There will be plants. There will be grain. There will be food. There will be flowers. There will be fruit. There will be a tomorrow.

Don't worry you are being taken care of and watched over. Relax and get in tune with God and each other and go for love walks . . . in the rain.

On Ritual and Ceremony

An ongoing series of heinous acts of terrorism and destruction recently have challenged the freedoms we hold to be our way of life. This attack has not just been inflicted on our beloved United States and its people, but upon the basic values of what free societies cherish around the world.

After decades of apathy and a general disdain for traditions. Immediately following the attacks, the people throughout the free world came together for comfort, to grieve, and to focus the scope of their emotions. Many found this in the ancient traditions of religious ritual. They congregated with people of like faith and practiced the religious ceremonies of that conviction.

For all appearances, the world had shifted to a more secular, individual leaning. I had come to believe that the "religion" of freedom, of self-importance, had replaced the necessity of our place within the rite. I was amazed and pleased to be proven wrong.

All this caused me to revisit an essay I had written a couple of years ago on "The Absence of Rituals and Ceremonies in America." In that text I visited the demise of the power of these sacramental exercises of responsibility to others, and pondered that dearth. There had been a stifling vacuum of meaning in life. People cried for the fresh air that the power of ritual brings but were not willing to accept that their grandmother's way was valid. The collective thought was that there must be a better way.

It appears that Grandmother was right.

With your permission, I would like to share the revision of that essay and a happening of great importance that occurred just this month. Megwich. (Thank you.)

The connection between community and ritual are inextricably intertwined.

Americans have nearly eliminated significant ceremony and ritual from our lives. Even in our religious lives, most of us only practice ritual during the high Holy Days of Rosh Hashana, Yom Kipper, Christmas, Easter, Ramadan, and others of each sect.

This is a sadness, a true shame.

Ceremony and ritual gives us an ability to be a part of a whole, a part of a meaning that others who think as us are embracing at the same time. These rituals were practiced by our grandparents, not out of blind obedience, but because they found great meaning in the observances of traditions that have been passed on to them for safe-keeping. There is satisfying and rewarding power in ritual that can be found in no other function of life.

No doubt they have been greatly disappointed and felt they were a failure to their faith as we have moved away from their practices and created new ones for ourselves.

This is reminiscent of the story of Moses when he had returned from the mountain with God's message, to find that his people had created new rituals in his absence. As history was to reveal, they paid dearly for their time of selfness. I do not believe that what happened on September eleventh was that of the Hand of God, but it was a shattering of our complacency and an awakening of our need for tradition.

America, and the free world have had a grand history of being a part of community, of caring for others. For well over two hundred years, various organizations, religious, fraternal and service clubs throughout the United States have offered their many rituals for their followers. These groups encompass a grand range from the devout clergy sects with their cloistered monasteries, to the

> To be human is to be truth, less will make us hollow.

outrageous who gather to create and bring life to floats at New Orleans' Mardi Gras. One of the common denominators is that they all hold ritual and ceremony to have significant meaning to their efforts. Traditional rites of prayer, grand pageantry, bowing and scraping, visitations at stations, of song, service to others in need, flag and ceremonial object honoring, of birth death marriage and death, of christening and burials, all ceremonial rituals.

During the last forty years, the brilliant light of many of these religious, fraternal organizations and service clubs—and their yeoman work—have diminished to a dim flicker. Before your breechcloth gets bunched, we are fully aware that the designation fraternal is a politically incorrect term today. Being PC is part of what is wrong today, live with it.

We have said time again, "Don't bother me with charity and good works, that is what we pay taxes to the government. It is their job. How self centered, how "me."

Perhaps now, as our country and its values are under attack, we should take a second look at these organizations.

Ah, but you say, "I belong to a church. We have our rituals of ceremony; isn't that enough?"

Well, frankly speaking, no.

Our faith in that great Power, that is detailed in our various religious doctrines, is of eternal value to each devout person. This is the reason for our belief. In my studies as a religious scholar, I have learned that one of the prime doctrines of all religions requires that we do good works for strangers, our neighbors and friends. The foundation of each of those religions teaches that this doctrine is of great importance. Again, the wisdom of the Elders of each group's origin holds in like-truth that doing the required acts, the rituals, is so significant.

Face it, we have been the generation of "me" . . . and we have taught our offspring the same. Even those who have been active in ritual and ceremony are more self-indulgent than the grandparents who gave us our traditional roots.

Isn't it time that we look to our center, our soul, and try to see what we have been missing?

The Reburial Ceremony

Recently my people, the Shawnee in Ohio, were confronted with a great responsibility to rebury some of our ancestors whose bones and artifacts had been exhumed in an archeological dig. These remains had lain untouched in a barn for nearly a half-century before a stranger, filled with compassion purchased at auction, twelve sealed cardboard boxes of American Indian remains. He contacted our tribe and made arrangements for us to rebury the "twelve ancestors" contained in the boxes.

It wasn't until he arrived at our Fall Council and we began the task of preparation for this ceremony, thatwe become aware of the true scope that this ritual would take.

Fall Council had been in session for little over an hour when they arrived. We had been expecting the boxes containing the twelve remains and were prepared for the ritual for reburial. Twelve excavations had been prepared in the traditional manner, the depth of a man at the waist. Red cloth was ready and items to accompany the remains as they continued their journey were prepared. Sage and sweetgrass and tobacco were gathered in bundles to make the smoke prayers for the ritual cleansing and in observance of our ancient customs.

Two long tables were set up and the women spiritual leaders were prepared for their tasks. In our tradition, the women of the family are responsible for the burial preparations.

One by one the old misshapen and stained cardboard boxes were removed from the truck in which they had made this part of their journey. The boxes were heavy and we wondered if there was still earth from the original burial sites in Ohio and Kentucky that had been removed with the bodies buried so long ago. The containers were placed in rows on one of the tables to be opened individually for the burial ceremony.

Sage was lit and each person in the ceremonial group "smugged." An attitude of respect and spirituality filled the tribal lands as we prepared for the task of re-interment at hand.

The ceremony for reburial is of a reasonable length, and we had prepared to make that span available at this time. But as we removed the bones and counted the remains in the first box, we were astounded to find that there were fourteen partial skeletons therein. Two more than we had expected overall. By the time we had opened and prepared the last of the twelve boxes, we had counted seventy-one adults and perhaps as many as twenty children and infants all removed from their burial sites in Ohio and Kentucky.

This was all ostensibly done for scientific study. In fact, they had lain in those sealed boxes for all these years with little evidence that they had even been revisited after the initial dig so many years ago.

I am a modern Indian man who understands the great vale we Indians have garnered from anthropological studies, no matter how reprehensible. This, however, astounded and angered me. I cannot conceive of a reason that these people had not been returned to the earth for their journey, save for the arrogance of a cult of scientists who feel their right to study supercedes the dignity of those interred.

I have tried to comprehend their motives. After that day, I no longer care about their motives. If you are not going to study a person's remains in the context of scientific discovery and have no end date to do so, then by God, leave them where they lay.

Have you no honor?

In all this, my People learned great and valuable lessons in the reburial of our ancestors. Because of the magnitude of this ceremony, the Spiritual leaders who commonly performed such acts were overwhelmed. Many who would have never come forward to take part in these rituals honored the ancestors by their participation.

It was an extraordinarily moving and important time in the life of these Shawnee People. As we learned these rituals, we became most aware of our responsibilities, and what is expected of us as we in turn hand to each generation what is required of them. The rituals of reburial, the Shawnee-way.

During the reburial, we did that which was right, and in so doing, did it in a good way. Each person in turn took part in the ritual, and the nearly one hundred Ancestors that we returned to the earth were honored in their passage to the other side. There were so many, yet we did our job as the ancestors expected.

We reverently wrapped the remains in good red cloth and made Smoke Prayers and said silent words of grief and joy as we prepared them for reburial. Tears flowed and emotions surfaced as we held the bones of each person for the time necessary to respectfully honor them as they continued their journey. We learned that they were much like us. Some were in good health, strong of bone and stature. Others suffered from arthritis and malnutrition. They were from all age groups, including some very aged Peoples. It is interesting to note that there were stone points with the remains. I wondered if they were burial items or the cause of their death. At last all the bundles were wrapped and the prayers said, and that part of the ritual was at an end. We carried the bundles to an awaiting vehicle and began the half-mile ritual walk to our Place for the Dead.

Following our Pipe Carriers and Ceremonial People, we formed a long cortege. We did them and ourselves honor as we carried their sacred bodily vestiges in the best way we knew. Each of us sang our Heart Songs, the special song each person chooses for our personal song, as we placed them once again into Grandmother's care. In this modern time, we performed the rituals in much the same way their grandparents did when they were first lain into the earth so many decades ago.

> Death is not the termination of of the book of life but a pause between chapters.

After the placing of the remains in the earth, we honored them as best we could with the gifts we had at that time. Our respect and dignity could not have been greater. As we performed the rituals, I am sure that our parents looked upon us and smiled. I believe that they felt proud of our efforts, as meager as they seemed to us. In the end, it was all about our trying. That is all it really is ever about.

Even with all that, we still did not keep the focus that the ceremony required. The task was a long process and it was arduous. There were moments when some broke away to talk of matters not related to the responsibility we had before us. We are children of this time, easily distracted from purpose. We have become a part of the instant society that craves for sound-bites and flash cards. We are not of the past, but of this time and place. So we deal with it with the skills at-hand.

Being Shawandasse today is so very different from the "other" world we live in daily. This takes patience and the persistence and serenity of our Ancestors, and of our Okeamas, the teachers, as we find our place within the eternal Circle. If we continue to try, we will, in the end, achieve what is expected. Each time we do these Honor Ceremonies, we learn more of our part in the Great Plan. As we learn from our Kitch Okeama, we learn how we will have to honor our Kitch Okeama when it is his time. We do not wait for that time, and we do not welcome it, but it will come. It comes for each of us. We need to be ready.

As you can see, even rituals long forgotten and never passed down have a way of regenerating themselves when it is time. We have seen this in the thousands of rituals and ceremonies that have taken place since September 11, 2001; including the names scrawled on the walls in memorial and the photos and teddy bears and messages of hope and grief, a ritual began in Oklahoma after the horrendous bombing of the Federal Building a few years ago.

We watch in silent horror as the rescue workers stop each time another body is found at Ground Zero. They pay tribute by draping the body in the Stars and Stripes, and as the remains are carried out, they form two lines facing the cortège and salute. We gather in small groups at churches and temples to return to the ritual, and by the hundreds of thousands to light candles and march or to raise monies at major events for the families of the victims.

The old ritual of baseball's "seventh inning stretch" has dropped its familiar songs like *Take Me Out to the Ball Game* and have replaced them with patriotic and inspirational tunes.

America is crying out for the return of ritual.

This is the time to see what you are really doing with your life. Set apart a piece of time where you are serving "me" . . . and work in some service projects with the neighbors and our community through the many available organizations. Join one of the organizations in your community and enjoy the fellowship of the ritual of singing friendship songs, offering pledges, and socializing. You will find solace. You will feel a sense of being a part of an entity than is greater that you. You will find that you truly care. These things are so very important.

If you have forgotten who these groups are, or never knew of them, locate, research, and join one of the following: Lions Club, Optimist Club, The Elks (BPOE), Kiwanis, Rotary, Soroptimist (for women), Eagles, Exchange Club, Junior League, Sertoma, Zonta . . . just look in your local directory or on the Internet under Community Service Clubs. Spend some time with your newfound group and participate.

I guarantee you will be a better human for this effort and you just might enjoy yourself at the same time. Now isn't that a better way to be kind to "me?"

Bring back ceremony and ritual to your life. It is so very important to be a part of good works at this trying place in our lives.

I am not simply being philosophical, but am confronting my challenges as realist. I perceive that it is our responsibility and our Path to be continued from the First Parents. It is simply our job.

That's What Grandmas are For

An email message for Jessica by *Lazorleter. Author unknown.*

"What you doing Grandma? Tell me now."
"Making a dream catcher. Here I'll show you how."

"Oh goodie, tell me again, too,
how my dream catcher will work and what it can do."

"I will my sweet, but first let's find feathers and beads
for color and some leather strips to bind.

"A hoop will be needed. Some webbing, too.
I know I have some. Ah! I think this will do.

"Now, my sweet, come sit by me.
You can do this, watch and see."

I sat and watched, with a shine in my eye.
Those tiny fingers, really, really try.

We talked of the web and what it will do.
It must be tight, and pretty, too.

The hole in the web, the strips that hang down,
and the reason it goes, round and round.

She chattered and worked, busy as a bee.
All at once, I looked and she was me!

Time flew and all too soon, the project done.
She gushed with delight, "Oh grams, that was fun!

"Can I take it next door," she smiled real wide,
"and show it to Katie?" She beamed with pride.

I said "Sure, my sweet, that's up to you.
You could even tell what a dream catcher will do."

As I watched her dash out the front door,
I said to myself "That's what Grandmas are for."

One cannot
be long angry
in the loving
arms of
another.

Dream Catcher

The following story is a combination of information gathered by Lyn Dearborn from California, Mary Ritchie of the Northern Woodlands, with assistance from Canadian elders, and with comments by Jim Great Elk Waters. Please visit www.nativetech.org/dreamcat/dreamcat for the complete article.

One of the cherished traditions of Native Americans is the dream catcher. We see them in every Indian shop, trading post, and at pow-wow's throughout North America. The dream catcher is one of the most recognizable objects in Indian culture. The Ojibwe (called Chippewa by others) originated the dream catcher. Variously named Asubakacin (As?ba' kasen Ojibwe—White Earth Band, meaning "net-like, looks like a net") and Bwaajige Ngwaagan (Bwa'sjg? Ngwä'jgn Ojibwe—Curve Lake Band, meaning "dream snare"), Today dream catchers are made by Native American artists from many Nations.

These light, airy frames that float above our beds, on rearview mirrors in our cars and trucks, and over baby cribs, are traditionally made of willow and sinew for children, and are not meant to last. The willow dries out and the tension of the sinew collapses the dream catcher. That's supposed to happen. It belies the temporariness of youth. Adults should use dream catchers of woven fiber, which is made up to reflect their adult "dreams." It is also customary in many parts of Canada and the Northeastern U.S. to have the dream catchers be a teardrop/snowshoe shape.

> No dream comes
>
> true unless
>
> you breathe
>
> into it life.

The dream catchers, representing spiderwebs, were usually hung from the hoop of a child's cradleboard, and it was said that "they catch and hold everything evil as a spider's web catches and holds everything that comes into contact with it." Dream catchers were wooden hoops filled with a web made of cord.

The Ojibwe tradition is told in story form. Long ago, in the ancient world of the Ojibwe Nation, the Clans were all located in one general area of that place known as Turtle Island. This is the way that the old Ojibwe storytellers say how Asibikaashi (Spider Woman) helped Wanabozhoo bring giizis (sun) back to the People. To this day, Asibikaashi builds her special lodge before dawn. If you are awake at dawn, as you should be, look for her lodge and you will see this miracle of how she captured the sunrise as the light sparkles on the dew which is gathered there. Asibikaasi took care of her children, the People of the land, and she continues to do so to this day.

When the Ojibwe Nation dispersed to the four corners of North America to fill a prophecy, Asibikaashi had a difficult time making her journey to all those cradle boards, so the mothers, sisters, and Nokomis (grandmothers) took up the practice of weaving the magical webs for the new babies using willow hoops and sinew or cordage made from plants in the shape of a circle to represent how giizis travel each day across the sky.

It is still held that dream catchers filter out all the bad bawedjigewin (dreams) and allow only good thoughts to enter into our minds when we are just abinooji. You will see a small hole in the center of each dream catcher where those good bawadjige may come through. With the first rays of sunlight, the bad dreams would perish.

When we see little asibikaashi, we should not fear her, but instead respect and protect her. In honor of their origin, the number of points where the web connected to the hoop numbered eight for Spider Woman's eight legs, or seven for the Seven Prophecies.

It was traditional to put a feather in the center of the dream catcher; it means breath, or air. It is essential for life. A baby watching the air playing with the feather on her cradleboard was entertained while also being given a lesson on the importance of good air. This lesson comes forward in the way that the feather of the owl is kept for wisdom (a woman's feather) and the eagle feather is kept for courage (a man's feather). This is not to say that the use of each is restricted by gender but that to use the feather, each is aware of the gender properties she/he is invoking. (Indian people, in general, are very specific about gender roles and identity.) The use of gemstones, as we do in the ones we make for sale, is not something that was done by the old ones. Government laws have forbidden the sale of feathers from our sacred birds, so using four gemstones to represent the four directions, and the stones used by western nations, were substituted by us.

The woven dream catchers of adults do not use feathers.

Now you know a bit about dream catchers. The next time you see one, you can share your knowledge with others. They will appreciate your gift.

Faith in the Family

I cannot speak for all the People of the Great Turtle Island but I will tell you of our spirit and Family connection, and I can safely say that many others here believe similarly. I will tell you of those who follow the Coashellaqua-way and Mide'-way.

For centuries we were called heathen savages by the newcomers, the invaders, but we were neither heathen nor savage. We have always, since the first parents, believed in a single Creator that we call Gieclamookalong, or He Who Creates with Thought. This Spirit is one and three the other two faces He offers are that of Kiji Manito and Nanabusho. Three and yet one. Strange? Haven't we heard that before somewhere?

We have always been centered in our faith and our family. In fact, our governmental organization is centered about the family circle rather than by region, as is usually the case.

The family makes up the Clan, a group of people living in one political government that are all related lineally to each other. You may never marry within your Clan, but all other Clans are now represented within your Clan by virtue of marriage of those outside your family group. All the Clans are then united into the Sept, or organization of all the related families. So you see, the family remains the center of our being.

And the same can be said for our Spirituality, our religious Faith. We have only one cardinal rule, one true commandment: Never let the People die. The People ARE the family. So: Never let the Family die. We traditionally have separated the acknowledgement of Creator's Gifts into two regions of learning—the Sky Grandfather or Kitch

Manitimussumtha, and the Earth Grandmother or Kohkumthena. Between their loving hands are where we are held.

In the Creation Process, Gieclamookalong once thought, "How will this Thing I have begun continue?" And at once there were all the first females of each species. And Creator was most pleased. But then He thought, "Who will care for my Creation Mothers?" And at once all the first males of each species began. So, as you see, all our Spirituality is centered within the family.

When we plan to do a new thing, we must ask, "How will this affect the next seven generations and the past seven generations?" And we are always offering our prayers to Creator for all our Relations, for all our Ancestors.

> Happiness, laughter and family voices in a home keep more people living right than all the laws man can make.

These things we know to be our truths. These things we know to be our Path to the Circle on the other side.

So, in summary, iIt is our very center to connect Creator and Family within the same Circle. It is our responsibility to live our lives in this relationship, and to teach our children to understand the same, for now, and for the next Seven Generations.

Adean: It is said, therefore it is.

Are We Still Here?

This is the question we feel is contemplated over and over again by the Ancestors as each new generation is born. It is believed that they seek to determine the simple fact: Have the Traditions been kept, or did they die with the last generation?

For tens of thousands of changing seasons, we have been guided by the Three Sisters of the Seven Stars in the winter sky. They have led us to the warm winter grounds and returned us to the warmth of summer's immeasurable bounty. In this endless cycle, we have found peace, harmony, and balance.

Once again, as winter enfolds us in its snowy embrace, all life begins to slow. This is as it should be. And as our Grandparents before us, we will take this time to finish the small tasks. By the fire, we can review the previous season of thirteen moons, remembering its greatness—and learning from the weakness.

It is the time for contemplation. Merged with our thoughts, our hands can complete the long deferred tasks that we have wanted to do during the warm months. Yes, He who Creates with His Mind gives us this time to repair and to prepare, to mend the breaks with Tradition, and make ready for our needs when next the world turns green.

> We cry for peace, but are we willing to accept it's compromise.

This is the time to make whole all which He first envisioned, when he Created us with His thought. To do less would unwrap the Bundle that is our destiny. We are like no others. We are connected to the First People by a single cord that is yet not broken. In this time of darkness, this long cold winter—it is with us now that the faith of All Our Relations has been placed.

Each spring, when the Ones Before Us awake, they ask, "Are we still here?"

Now it is our time. Now the children of the First People are to spin the next length of the Cord of Existence. Wrap your strength, your fiber, your very being into the dreams of our ancestors add to it your vision and become one with All People of All Time.

When we next visit, we will see how long the Cord will be for the next thirteen moons . . . and will be able to assert that, "We are still here!" I live for that moment.

Are You an Indian?

This story provided by Les Tate of the Tennessee Valley Authority, November 18, 1996. Published in the back pages of Chautauqua— Echoes in the Wind, *July 20, 1997. Author Unknown.*

How often have you heard or said, "I'm part Indian?" If you have, then some Native American elders have something to teach you. A very touching example was told by a physician from Oregon who discovered as an adult that he was part Indian. This is his story. Listen well.

Some twenty or more years ago, while serving the Mono and Chukchanse and Chownumnee communities in the Sierra Nevada, I was asked to make a house call on a Mono elder. She was 81 years old and had developed pneumonia after falling on frozen snow while bucking up some firewood.

I was surprised that she had asked for me to come since she had always avoided anything to do with the services provided through the local agencies. However, it seemed that she had decided I might be alright because I had helped her grandson through some difficult times earlier, and had been studying Mono language with the second graders at North Fork School.

She greeted me from inside her house with a Mana' hu, directing me into her bedroom with the sound of her voice. She was not willing to go to the hospital like her family had pleaded, but was determined to stay in her own place and wanted me to help her using herbs that she knew and trusted, but was too weak to do alone. I had learned to use about a dozen native medicinal plants by that time, but was inexperienced in using herbs in a life or death situation. She eased my fears with her kind eyes and gentle voice. I stayed with her for the next two days, treating her with herbal medicine (and some vitamin C that she agreed to accept).

She made it through, and we became friends. One evening several years later, she asked me if I knew my elders. I told her that I was half Canadian and half Appalachian from Kentucky.

> We are the total sum of all our Ancestors.

I told her that my Appalachian grandfather was raised by his Cherokee mother, but nobody had ever talked much about that and I didn't want anyone to think that I was pretending to be an Indian. I was uncomfortable saying I was part Indian and never brought it up in normal conversation.

"What! You're part Indian?" she said. "I wonder, would you point to the part of yourself that's Indian. Show me what part you mean."

I felt quite foolish and troubled by what she said, so I stammered out something to the effect that I didn't understand what she meant. Thankfully, the conversation stopped at that point. I finished bringing in several days' worth of firewood for her, finished the yerba santa tea she had made for me, and went home still thinking about her words.

Some weeks later, we met in the grocery store in town and she looked down at one of my feet and said, "I wonder if that foot is an Indian foot. Or maybe it's your left ear. Have you figured it out yet?"

I laughed out loud, blushing and stammering like a little kid. When I got outside after shopping, she was standing beside my pick-up, smiling and laughing. "You know," she said, "you either are or you aren't. No such thing as part Indian. It's how your heart lives in the world, how you carry yourself. I knew before I asked you. Nobody told me. Now don't let me hear you say you are part Indian anymore."

She died last year, but I would like her to know that I've heeded her words. And I've come to think that what she did for me was a teaching that the old ones tell people like me, because others have told me that a Native American elder also said almost the same thing to them. I know her wisdom helped me to learn who I was that day, and her words have echoed in my memory ever since. And because of her, I am no longer part Indian, I *am* Indian.

How Can You Be an American Patriot and a Good Indian?

This is a subject that often comes up in Indian Country, and it divides us.

There are three general camps that have polarized the American Indian. First there are the "Traditional Indians," who would have life as it was BWM, (before white man). They run the gamut from the militant AIM to the families far back in the hills or the outreaches of the reservations who just want to be left alone. The second are the people who have given up all "Indian-ness" and live their lives without any semblance of being Indian. Many in this sector were disenfranchised by their parents or grandparents who either hid their heritage or dismissed it, to be assimilated into mainstream America during the 1920s and '30s. And then there is the major body of what makes up the American Indian today. They are simply American Indians who accept being American, who live their lives in the Indian-way within the framework of the laws and traditions of the United States today.

All three groups are Indians. They can be found across the spectrum of the people who are the descendants of the First Americans.

Recently, I had a heated discussion with a dignified Native American statesman. He proclaimed that he would not rest until the "land is returned."

"What land?" I asked.

> Patriotism is birthed in the concept of humility, and of the realization that your single voice is the power of the Nation itself.

"The land that was stolen from us," he replied in a solemn tone.

"Oh my, someone has taken your land?" I asked. "Did you report this to the police?"

In an exasperated tone, he replied, "No! It was taken a long time ago."

The discussion continued until he said, "You know, it was the land that belonged to our People before the white man came here."

We had arrived at the base of his complaint.

I politely reminded him that he could not own something that he never possessed. We talked of the Indian concept of land ownership, that the land was for all the people, not individuals or tribes. That traditionally, we would live upon a piece of land until it no longer supported our needs, then we moved to another unoccupied place to make our home. In this way, we allowed the land to heal, and ensured that in time it would regenerate naturally for others.

We spoke of his perception that our land had been stolen, and I reminded him that our ancestors suffered invasions by foreigners and that we lost the battles, and the wars. The invaders attempted in many ways to assimilate us into their way of life, but were not successful. Today we have retained much more of our culture and tradition than nearly all the other conquered indigenous peoples around the world.

Yes today's Indian-way is different than that of our great grandparents, but their way of life had evolved from that of their great grandparents, also. Our traditions have never been a catscan slice of our history at a moment in time. One time, long ago, we hunted the saber-toothed tiger and the mastodon; then came the elk and the buffalo; and today, we do our hunting and gathering in the modern equivalents of the forest and streams—the K-marts and the A&Ps. Indian-life has always been an evolving, living organism that grows and adapts to each succeeding generation.

The "old days" never existed in the way that most of us perceive them, and few of us would want to live in that manner. Even if we had won the wars and repelled the invaders, we still would have been a people of the earth, and civilization would have progressed in a similar manner. There is no doubt that the great Chiefs and Spiritual leaders of the tribes of yesterday would have adapted today's societal advantages. They would have cars and houses and televisions and computers, just like they do today. We are an opportunistic people who have forever adapted to change.

Look around, my brothers and sisters. This nation of many nations offers us more, respects us in a better way, considers us a part of the whole than nearly any other victor-nation worldwide. America, in general, allows us the freedom to be who we are, even if we do not fit nicely into their grand plan. We can still practice our religion and our traditions, within bounds. We cannot forget that there was a time not too long in the past when our parents and grandparents faced another set of rules.

That was then, this is now.

Today we are American citizens, American Indians living in a strong, free society. As long as we do not break the laws, we are able to live like any other American.

It is a fact that the Americans gave up much of their Eurocentric practices and adopted much of our Indian form of life. Our government today is based, in great part, on the representative democracies that our ancestors enjoyed. Their Clans are our States, their Councils are our Legislative bodies, their Chiefs our Governors and the President, and the wisdom of the Elders is our Judicial system. In the time before Columbus got lost and "found" us, our relatives were free to live where they pleased. So are we. The way of our ancestors is alive and well today in America.

Yes, there are many unjust things that still need to be addressed and corrected, but today we are far better than many of our ancestors. Don't kid yourselves, they would have traded with us at the first hard freeze or season of famine.

The truth is that we will never be able to live as our ancestors. We will never live in a land where there are just Indian People. But, we will be able to live safer, free from invasions, be healthier, not worry about famine and cold, and be successful in our chosen endeavors. We live secure in the fact that due to the great combined strengths of the many states in this United States, we will, for the foreseeable future, be able to enjoy all this as we see fit.

We are free Indians living in the land of the greatest freedoms in the world.

If none of this persuades you, perhaps a quote from Panther in the Sky by James Alexander Thom might ease your pain a smidgen.

> " . . . the attitude of the red man towards his home-land was never obvious to Anglo-Americans . . . a compassionate, liberal-minded white man and a Shawnee veteran of Viet Nam, had been conversing earnestly for hours (when) my fellow white man shook his head and blurted, "But, my God! How can you go and fight a war for a country that's treated your people the way it has?" The Shawnee smiled and wagged his head slowly. He put his fist against the man's knee, chuckled and said, "You palefaces still can't understand that this is our country, can you?"

(That decorated Shawnee veteran who survived Nam, Yahma Walter Shepherd, is at this writing fighting to survive the cancer, leukemia.)

Addressing the past is an ongoing problem that needs to be attended to in a logical manner. Do not misunderstand my position, the passionate warrior in me wants retribution, but the realist cries out, "We can't change the past."

The crimes committed by others in the past cannot be corrected or atoned for by anyone today. The many who would apologize and offer compensation have no connection with the horrors that were visited on our grandparents' grandparents. Unless the perpetrators are still alive (in which case there should be no statute of limitations) to be held accountable, then it is really meaningless for anyone else to "apologize" for things they never did. Yes, I understand that governments are still in place, but as in the case of the Indian-way being a growing organism, America is a similar living entity. Governments before this one have addressed the problems of genocide and enslavement and terror, and have ended those heinous practices.

What should America do for the Indian?

No apology would correct or remove the pains suffered from past transgressions.

The America of past generations has participated in so many terrible wrongs, that the only way to truly right those wrongs would be to disenfranchise the nation and form a new one. Not going to happen.

Can we realistically compensate monetarily or physically for the wrongs done? There is not enough wealth or property to adequately make things right.

The acts of history are done. They cannot be reversed. Our laws have been changed. There is nothing more to be done that will make a real difference.

It is time that we, who have had wrong things done to our race, ethnicity, sex, ancestors, etc. (which is about all humans), accept that the past is carved in stone, un-erasable, yet never to be forgotten. We need to draw a line at this moment, stating that we will never allow that to happen again.

It is time we quit making ourselves victims of the past and take our rightful place in the present, building a future where the past wrongs will not have a place to occur again.

So, have I answered, "How can I be an American Patriot and a good Indian?" If not, there is little use in discussing it more. However, I have adopted a new philosophy.

"Live in the present, be ever-watchful, quit whining, and Grow Up!"

At least that is my plan.

Through the Veil

Written shortly after my father, Okema Ten Moons, passed through the Veil, to ease my spirit's great pain.

The hollowness of being alone when our mortal love for another finds that two-legged no longer here to receive our gift, is at once loneliness absolute, inconsolable by any wisdom. Only time may provide passage to release this pained wanting. Only familiarity of times past will give ease, with its shared remembrances of all things common, now so significant.

> Everyone fears death until they possess that which lives after death.

The remembered emotions shared become sands to be poured freely into the abyss to replace the pain of our great loss, and it is the slow acceptance of the Spirit Walk that softens reality's edge. The gentle gift of the Old Ones gives us direction in this place, serves as the firm support on which to rebuild the shattered lodge of our lives when one of the main poles of life travels on.

It is told that when we go to the dream sleep ending our two-legged walk on the Good Red Road journey, we step through the Veil into the place where All Our Relations have been waiting. This is the next step on the long trail to reach the Balance that the Great Creator, Kitch Gieclamookalong, envisioned when first we were begot by Creator's Thoughts, and it is the reality of our existence.

Thus, when we feel the emptiness of our reflected love for those who have gone to be with the Ancestors, feel no sorrow for they have found that which we have yet to become the Balance Creator envisioned when each being first became Manitou's Thought.

6   For the Joy of It All

They are singing song of the earth. I love hearing the children's voices sing these songs.

Lela Fisher, Hoh Elder
From *Through Indian Eyes*

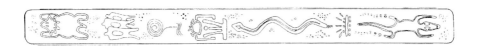

OS TOH WEH GO WAH

GREAT FEATHER DANCE

With Best Wishes
To "SAH-NEE-WEH"
Beaver Clan

Drawing By 1st
"HA YONH" Snipe Clan
Jesse J Cornplanter 1936

A'ho, Let's go Powwow!

There are few events that are as fun as a powwow, but they can be intimidating. If you don't know what is happening and you "make a mistake," your day could be ruined. No one wants this, so I have gathered some information together on powwows. These are based on my general knowledge and on program guides I have collected from events around the country.

Let's have fun!

We can all recall the lasting memories of our first powwow.

The powerfully mystical, exciting vision of swirling feathers; the flight of fringed leather and bright colors as the sounds of the drum ring in our ears; and the aroma of fry bread served with honey or made into "Indian Tacos" with chili, cheese, onions and tomatoes. Can't you taste them now? All the intoxicating ambiance of the power of a powwow combine to transport us to a make-believe world.

Make believe? Yes, at least at urban powwows.

Today, there are two distinctly different styles of events. Those held on Tribal Lands are embedded in the traditions of that People, and are the outward celebration of their culture. The urban powwow is an event, a gathering if you will, of a grand mix of diverse tribal cultures and traditions competing for the same honor. Here, the ceremonies have little similarity to those of our ancestors.

The urban powwow today has become a "pan-Indian" compilation of bits and pieces of many Native American cultures. They are blended into a blur that really represents no one ideology. I don't say this in a disrespectful way, but to point out that the ceremonies at powwows today have little resemblance to those of our grandparents. The pow-wow has evolved to become the American Indian's "Pleasure Faire." This is good and proper, just not truly authentic.

The urban powwow is, by its nature, an intensely competitive happening. Here, it is terribly easy to offend another. Indians from different places around the country have different beliefs. Some dance with the clock (clockwise) and others the opposite. At the Tribal pow-wow, everyone knows which way that group dances, and there is no problem; but at urban events, we need to respect and honor the head-man's instructions and temporarily change our way, if necessary. Remember, you are their guest. This is good, the modern Indian-way.

All this said, if you can accept the changes and are careful not to step on anyone's toes, you can have a great time at an urban powwow.

What exactly is a powwow?

Powwow is a time when Native Americans gather for fellowship and dance. A time for renewing acquaintances and to make new friends along the way. Here, we remember the old ways and through these "pan-Indian" celebrations, we continue our heritage of connectedness. Many of the participants, the dancers, singers, announcers, and vendors, are a part of the "powwow circuit." Like a rodeo troupe, these families follow the schedule of powwows around the country.

For first time visitors, this is a wonderful time to meet and learn of "Indian Ways." The primary concern here is to be respectful. Listen, observe, and participate. You will have a wonderful time. Here are some thoughts on the aspects of the powwow that will make your attendance an unforgettable and exciting experience.

Listen and Learn

The first thing to learn is to listen to the announcers and the Master of Ceremonies. Every powwow has a person or persons who serve in these capacities. They keep the pace flowing, introducing events, announcing the dances, who may dance and when. They fill the air with banter and tidbits of knowledge, joking and cajoling, telling lost parents where to find their charges. In general, they are your best source of powwow etiquette. Please pay attention to make sure you do not offend others or embarrass yourself. Enough said.

Arena Directors: The Arena Directors are most often honored dancers. Their job is to keep the order of drums and dance contests coordinated and on scheduled. Of course always remember that most powwows run on "Indian Time." This means that although the events are intended to run at a specific time, at a powwow they are always flexible due to the informal nature of such diverse and large gatherings. Everything will start, and end, just not perhaps as posted. Be patient and enjoy the relaxed atmosphere.

Dance Arena: The Dance Arena is a large area, able to accommodate all the dancers and singers and observers, and may be outside or indoors. Before the event begins, the arena is blessed by an honored Elder or spiritual leader and is considered a sacred place for the time it is used as a dance arena.

The Arbor: There is an arbor for the drum, the singers and dancers, and their families. The Elders are always honored with the best seats along the arena.

The area around and inside the Dance Arena is not a playground. Adults are responsible for their children's actions. It is a no-no to run and play here and it is improper for viewers to cross the arena. If you are invited, always enter the arena respectfully and walk in a clockwise direction.

Take a seat in the bleachers, sit in your lawn chairs, or stand where the Arena Director indicates around the arena. If there are blankets on the bleachers, these are reserved. This may seem obvious, but it is not acceptable to sit on another's blanket unless you are invited. Be aware of those about you and try not to block their view. There is room for everyone at a powwow.

Now we are all seated and ready for the events.

You take out your camera to snap some memorable shots of the powwow. There is a dancer in a beautiful outfit who is preparing to dance, and you focus in.

Wait.

Did you ask permission of the Arena Director and the person you are photographing? It is powwow etiquette to get permission first, and you are almost never told no. So be courteous and ask. It is always acceptable to photograph groups without permission. If in doubt, ask.

During all Memorial or Honor Dances, please put down your camera.

Head Man, Head Woman, and Head Singer: Within the order of the performers and guests, there are special people known as "Head People." They are honored not only for their skills but also for the quality of person they are and how they respect others. The Head Man and Head Woman begin dancing to each song. They also direct the other dancers who respectfully wait until the Head Dancers begin.

Head Singer: There is also a Head Singer. It is a distinct honor to be chosen as Head Singer. This person must know all the songs, be able to lead the singing, and either starts the drum-singing or appoints a "lead" singer for this honor. All others wait for the signal to join in.

The Drum: The Drum is composed of beaters who drum and sing, and sometimes additional singers. Each Drum usually includes five to ten members. Sometimes they are entire families. They sing a variety of songs to allow dancers to show their distinctive styles. The singers are talented artists who are most important in today's culture. Singers offer fast and slow songs, grass dance shake and crow hops, and, of course, the popular sneak-ups. At one time they used to sing their Tribe's original songs in their native tongue, but as various tribes gathered for powwow, they would often change the words of their songs to vocables (wordless rhythmic intonations) so singers of different tribes could join in. Many of today's songs use only vocables. These are still special songs to the singers.

The Drum is Sacred: The drum is not an instrument or toy. It is a sacred connection to the traditional Indian way of life. All singers must know the drum protocol. It is cared for in a certain prescribed manner established by the traditions of the drum's origin. The drum is the rhythm of the dance and song. There are different types of drums used at powwows, but all drums are accorded the highest respect.

Just as with photography, recording the drum must be done only with the permission of the Master of Ceremonies and each drum's Head Singer.

Do not hang around a drum to get your recording. Be respectful.

Dancers: The performers seen at powwow today dancer mostly to "social" dances which, differ from traditional dances. Many of these modern steps are modified from the traditional dances, or have been created for the songs of today. The dance patterns and steps may have changed, however, their importance has not.

Invitations to Dance: You may be invited to dance with the dancers. This is an honor; but if you are not wearing traditional clothing, you should only dance to social songs like the two-step, blanket and honor songs.

If you are asked to dance by an Elder, he or she considers you special. Dance. Don't disrespect them and yourself by turning down this opportunity to learn how to dance.

This is a moment you will never forget.

There are many different types of dances. There are the inter-tribals that are the "everyone dance" styles for everyone of all ages and sex. The

MC will call, "Everyone dance; all you dancers, lets get out there!" There are several special songs performed at powwow. For these songs, it is tradition to stand. Men should remove their hats in respect, unless they are in traditional regalia. These songs are the Grand Entry, Flag Songs, Invocation, Memorial, Honor, Veterans Song, and Closing Song.

No one is to enter the dance circle unless they are dancing; this includes your children.

Grand Entry: In the Grand Entry, the dancers' parade leads off each session of the powwow. This is just as its name implies—a grand parade of the Elders, powwow leaders, VIPs, dancers who are contestants, and invited guests. It has all the power of the opening ceremonies at the Olympics, except this is for Indians to show their expertise in dancing and the regalia they wear. It is truly spectacular.

Flag and Honor Songs: These are very special songs. During the Flag and Honor Songs, it is proper for everyone to stand and remove their hats to show respect for the American flag and those who are honored.

Flag Song: Today about every Indian Nation has a Flag Song, which is sung at the beginning of most Native American events. It is dedicated to the men and women who have served in the armed forces, our warriors of today. Flag Songs are the Indian equivalent of our National Anthem. There is no dancing to this song. Women whose father, brother, or son is, or was a combat veteran may traditionally dance in place.

Honor Song and Veterans Song: Honor songs are always announced. They are to pay respect to particular people. Just as with the Flag Song, when these songs are performed, please stand in silence to show respect.

Round Dance: In this social dance, the dancers side-step in rows of circles clockwise around the arena, with the faster moving line close to the drum and the slower outside. The entire line moves as one body, in rhythm with the drum.

Two Step and Rabbit Dance: These are fun dances and two of the few where men and women dance as partners.

The Rabbit Dance comes from the Northern Plains tribes. The Two-Step is usually done as a part of the Rabbit Dance. Women choose their partners with couples holding hands. They circle the drum, stepping off with the left foot and dragging the right up with it in time to the drum. At traditional events, if a man refuses to dance, he has to "pay" (money or craft gift) the woman who asks him to dance. Don't dishonor the woman who asks you, dance—it is much fun.

Blanket Dance: The Blanket Dance is used to collect donations for the drum or other charitable causes. You are encouraged to enter the dance to donate, but use the east "door" or entrance only.

Giveaway: Sometimes during a powwow, there will be a Giveaway Dance where a distribution of goods by a family to friends, relatives, and visitors, is done in honor of a person or event. This is done to memorialize a death, a naming ceremony, or an adoption. The items in a Giveaway can be blankets, food, horses covered with money, or personal items of meaning to the giver. The giveaway is announced and is preceded by an Honor Song.

Gourd Dance: During Gourd Dancing (if any), only Gourd Dancers and Gourd Dance Societies are allowed to enter the Arena. Just having a gourd rattle does not make you a Gourd Dancer. Check with the local societies or the MC.

War Dance: There are also the War Dances. In the time before the wars between America and the many Indian Nations ended, this ceremony was restricted to only the best warrior dancers. Today this is a Plains Indians' victory dance, which is purely social and dignified, not violent as you would believe.

Snake Dance: The Snake Dance is where the dancers make the journey of a snake across the land. Coiling and uncoiling, the dancers finally cross back over the entire line, back to the tail (last) dancer. This dance is especially fun.

Flags and Regalia

Indian Flags: An Indian flag is a staff of a spiritual nature, covered in fur, and hung with feathers and other adornments. It represents the Indians and their Tribe. This staff is carried with honor by a veteran during the opening ceremonies.

Regalia: These clothes are not costumes. They represent our Spiritual connection to the dance and our traditions. It is not proper to touch a Regalia without the owner's permission. If you notice that we use modern equipment like safety pins and other "new" items. It is because we are a "living culture" and we adapt to the time in which we live. We are not re-creationist or reenactment groups, but are American Indians doing what we do best today.

Not All Indians Look Alike.

Leave your stereotype at home. Like any other ethnic group, we differ widely in our appearance and dress. Yes, there are even some Indians who are blond and/or have light colored eyes. We are the result of five hundred years of living and making families with people from other regions of the globe. We are modern Americans.

Live with it. We do!

The powwow is a time of joyful gathering and celebration of life. Most all powwows don't allow drugs or alcoholic beverages. Nearly half of Native Americans are diabetics, and a similar number suffer from substance dependency. Do the numbers. It is our number one problem in Indian Country. These elements have destroyed much our of way of life and thus are not welcome at powwows.

Don't embarrass your mothers. They taught you better, so pick up behind yourself. Isn't it disgraceful how much trash we people drop on the ground? Make an extra effort to hit the trash can.

Respect Grandmother Earth!

Native American Dances are more than just a dance. They are our ceremonies and prayers that encompass much of our lifestyle. We get enormous emotional and spiritual value from the dance. Some are old, some are brand new. Our culture lives and evolves.

All persons not in Regalia are asked to cover their legs before entering the dance arena. (Hint, no shorts.)

Please remember that these are general rules. There can be many other rules that are special to a particular event. They are usually posted or are in the program for you to read. Read and heed.

Above all, do have fun. Don't be uptight. Relax. Buy from the vendors. Donate if you can. The universe comes together at powwows to celebrate. Join in!

Now, lets go powwow!

Bird Dog

Indians have hunted with domesticated dogs for a very long time. There have been camp dogs and personal pets among the Indians from first history. The bonds between hunter and dog have been as close as any ever made. The dog is an extension of the hunter and many believe that the dog reads the hunter's mind and then acts accordingly. The stories of the hunt have been told around the campfires of generations upon generations to bring mirth into an otherwise hard life.

I get great joy in sharing this story of my Shawnee Elder brother and his bird dog experience in the field.

My older brother, Web "Kep" Kepish, has always been a hunter, and a good one. He has put meat on the table, when needed, since we were children. He is good with a bow and excellent with cartridges and black powder. But, he is not a sport hunter; he uses all he takes or shares, as is appropriate. Kep is also my best friend and hero. But this story is about neither.

To set the scene, we need to go back to the seventies, in rural Southern Ohio. Web has spent much of his time in the country. He says, "Musta been born in the wrong century." Probably a truth about many of our peers. Being a traditional Indian in this half of the twentieth century has been problematic.

This day was like it must have been back in the "eighteen hundreds" as Kep took his prize brindle Irish Pointer (Babe) out to the field. Babe was acknowledged by hunters far afield as a Queen of the Birders. She was the dread of nature's wild feathered creatures, for she could find, point, and flush the most recalcitrant bird in the county.

This day, the fall air was crisp and steam traveled off Babe's coat as she began working the
ground for wild grouse. She entered the field
with a dedication unique to her breed. She
explored remaining stems and flower heads of
the lushness of the summer past, searching for a
scent.

Darting cross-field in calculated abandon,
only stopping to raise her head high, Babe
methodically closed the field. She worked the
back high grasses for any trace of fowl. She
moved at a measured pace across the expanse
until at last she had neared a limestone bench.
This outcrop was at the end of the tree line near
the step that led to the cliffs beyond.

> Fire embers in
> campfire
> reflecting the
> star-filled sky
> and a trusty
> friend bring
> day's end into
> balance.

Although this was a great place for grouse to roost or hide, it
appeared that all the birds had left the roost.

This day it seemed, Kep would have to be satisfied with a stray rabbit or squirrel for the pot. Not what he had promised himself earlier
that morning.

The thought of that was sure to bring on one of his famous
"grumps."

If he had only gotten an earlier start. If only . . . But that was a
moot point as he had been forced to take valuable hunt-time to thaw
a waterline that had frozen overnight.

He knew that this was going to be a hard winter and there was a
lot of preparation ahead. Hunt or no hunt, the pipes had to be cared
for or he would spend the winter replumbing the place.

It was no boon that the first hard freeze had come near a month
early. This was going to be a long cold winter. He still had the last of
the potatoes and squash in the field and hay to loft . . .

With all this on his mind, Kep had completely forgotten Babe. As he looked about for the dog, Babe was not to be seen.

In this pastoral vista of beige and tan, the brindle-colored hound had disappeared into the wash of like-colors.

Kep put his cupped hands to his face, took the last finger of each to his lips, and sounded a sharp trill.

"Twerrrrippppppttt!"

The whistled notes echoed off the valley walls to either side and then fell silent. The songbirds that had been chatting and trilling ceased. There was nary a whisper of a breeze and the leaves hung motionless in the air. The meadow was bereft of sound. No movement was evident, save for a startled cardinal that flew wavelike into the trees.

Just as he was about to whistle again, he spied Babe.

She was near the edge of the meadow and was on full point. Nose, ears, and tail made a straight line aiming at an invisible target not twenty feet in front of her. The intended flush was hunkered down just beneath the stone shelf.

Now I need to tell you that Babe, although one of the great birders of the area, was not the most patient player in the field. She was easily the dog with the least patience in the county when a bird was want to stand its ground. Here, she showed her one great fault.

Babe began to creep forward.

Step at a time, she moved forward, and then on point. Still there was no bird. She continued, step, point, step, point until she had closed the distance from the bench to less than five feet.

I suppose that what happened next was partly caused by Babe's bad habits, as well as the natural action of a grouse being flushed. Irrespective of the reason, one moment there was dead silence and the next, utter pandemonium!

There had indeed been an old hen hunkered under the outcrop, and she had just about had enough of Babe's wet nose and Purina breath.

The bird took the path of least resistance and bolted. Right up the dog's nose, across her still board-stiff back, the bird launched her body skyward from the dog's haunches.

In a moment, the bird had reached the trees and safety.

Babe, being totally defeated in the hunt and now completely frustrated, ran in circles barking at the now empty rock outcropping, and then the place where she last saw the grouse in the tree line. After several turns at flank speed, Babe stopped, lowered her head, and lay in the now trampled meadow grass, and sulked.

Now if you ever saw a dog sulk, you can appreciate that this was the sulk of all sulks. Babe knew she had been bested by a dumb bird. I suppose that she was also considering that the grouse was still sitting in the trees, holding hard onto its perch to keep from falling as it laughed at this one dumb "bird dog" she had just trashed. It was more than Babe could endure. She closed her eyes and hoped that this would all go away.

Kep had seen where the dog had collapsed and waited. He knew that the hound's pride had been destroyed. Finally, with much coaxing, Babe came back to his feet, belly low to the ground and head lower. Her nose and back showed blood where the ol' hen had clawed her way to freedom.

It was clearly an end to the hunt that day. Dog and man went home, beaten in their singularly dejected state of mind.

Remember Babe's one bad habit, creeping up on her quarry?

The dog had learned a valuable lesson that day, and it was soon to be apparent that she had learned it all too well.

The next morning at sunrise, Kep and Babe prepared for another hunt. This time there were no delays, and Kep was out the door with coffee in-hand and Babe at his heels as the sun began its climb from the horizon into the clear autumn air. Soon they were in the field and on hunt.

Babe hadn't worked a quarter of the area before she had flushed several birds, and Kep had done his job well with six plump grouse.

Just then Babe went on point. Must be a big one, Kep thought, as he raised his gun to shoulder.

Then it happened.

As she had always done, Babe took her first single step. This time it was, well backwards, away from the bird at point. Then she took another step backwards. Step by step she moved farther from the prey until she nearly backed into Kep's leg.

No flushed grouse. All that remained of the hunt was a "grouse-shy" bird dog.

Any hunter worth his salt knows a dog that can't flush is worthless.

Time after time Kep took Babe back to the field, always with the same results. At last, he could no longer stand the embarrassment of it all and decided to be rid of Babe. He thought of just putting her down, but his fond recall of her better hunting days wouldn't allow that.

So he sold her to the people down the road. They had kids that wanted a house dog. An ignominious end to the once, "Queen of the Birders." Babe had been relegated to a "play-fetch" puppy with kids.

Such are the happenings, good and bad, of which life is made.

The sad part was that after a lifetime of grouse hunting, my brother had somehow lost some of his zeal to field a dog. I don't recall he ever sought grouse again with a dog. I suppose he just didn't want to be forced to recall the day that impulsive ol' hen grouse had ruined the best darned bird dog in this century, the "Queen of the Birders."

He still keeps a picture of Babe, to this day, in the desk drawer at home.

Night Flight

Early dawn's final approach ending another transcontinental flight as I once again travel to the homeland of the Shawnee for my tribal responsibilities. The great War Chief and Shawnee hero Tecumseh had visions of flight. I suppose my air sojourns would have Tecumseh's image of flight. I love to fly, but still find the magic of it all to be near overwhelming at times. Thus, Night Flight!

Cobalt chases indigo
as first light brings
clouds gray white
once hidden in dark.
The dome of eternal black
is filled still
with pricks of light
in all its immenseness.

Clouds, now silk soft
like milkweed,
lay close below
in undulation.
Seem firm, known not.

Now wisps bump
and float quick
against the wing
as we move faster
than prudent.

More gray-white forms
cause our gliding
birdlike machine
to slide to side,
pendulum free.

The lights of dark
disappear.
Yielding vapors
close about us
and at last
we are released.

On top of the bottom
of the Sky World
we fall to the line
of blue lights below.

In last second correction,
turbines wail.

Five, twenty knots.
Now,
Bump, scream, roar.

We slow to sanity
as if a miracle
at the end
of the blue lights.
Mach one ended . . .

I breathe.

Go Carefully

Author Unknown . . .

Aya-angwa-a'mizin is drawn from the Algonquian language.

Translated literally, it is usually read as "to go carefully," "to tread carefully."

But beyond this superficial meaning is the idea that the actions of persons have consequences for a larger whole. The term is used in a context that assumes the meaningfulness of existence and action, that we do not live in a "neutral" universe that exists beyond and outside ourselves. We are a part of the fabric of the universe.

All things are connected.

Puffer and the Mountain Lion

Some years ago, being cursed with the Shawnee nomadic nature to move to a new hunting ground (who says genetics don't play a role in life), we decided to move from Ohio to California.

We wanted to take the train west as our household was being shipped via freight. The only complication was a German shepherd named Puffer, a name derived from her fluffy white fur that reminded us of a powder puff. She was the family pet and Amtrak didn't allow dogs in the Pullman. We just couldn't think of letting her stay in the baggage car.

Therefore we devised a plan for me to drive ahead in our 1969 Fiat 124 Sports Coupe with Puffer to Los Angeles, get a job, establish a residence, and send for the family. Ah, I just love plans, don't you?

Puffer was a well-disciplined, happy dog that loved car rides. Her favorite pastime was to bark at cows, squirrels, butterflies, and any wildlife along the way. All we would have to say is, "Puffer, cows," and she would go on point, with the requisite bark, bark, bark. This would be her longest trip in a car, ever.

In truth, I was pleased that Puffer was to accompany me on the long drive. She would be "someone to talk with" and cause me to stop for rest breaks along the way. So, with the trunk packed to near bursting (we are not talking about a very large trunk here), and the back seat loaded to the window sills, we were off.

I had laid a blanket over the load on the backseat for Puffer's bed. But as you who live with dogs know, she spent most of the time in the passenger seat, on guard for the occasional cow or horse around the bend. In all, it was a great arrangement.

It was late in the evening on the third day, and we were driving the final miles along the south rim of the Grand Canyon. We were near the lodge that was to be our home for that night. It had been snowing steadily most of the day and there was two-foot of snow along the sides of the road. The plow had just recently cut a new path, and we were pro- ceeding at a leisurely pace of 15-20 mph, at best, on the fresh blanket of white. The snow falling in our headlights ahead looked like tiny cotton balls gently floating to join the sea of soft white fluff.

It was here, in this most peacefully enchanting scene, that it happened!

Almost as if by magic, a large shadow bounded into the roadway and stopped. I slowed the Fiat to a crawl and flashed my lights, to no avail. The large mass of beige fur simply stood its ground, fully blocking the only lane of plowed snow. As we got closer, I could see it was a moun- tain lion, a huge cat with a tail nearly as long as its body. Its tail lay on the snowbank on one side and its nose was close to the other side. This was a big cat.

Yes, you guessed it. Puffer also saw it, and here is where the situation escalated dramatically—and quickly.

Lion or not, to Puffer, this was a cat! Immediately she went on point as best she could in the car. I suppose her only thought was to tree this cat as she did the cats and squirrels back home. Barking and lunging, she was a fireball of comments that would not be satisfied until the cat was treed or disappeared.

Meanwhile, the giant puma had taken particular notice of the too-bright lights with the noisy, angry dog voice, turned with a snarl and with a raised paw. There was no way this cat was going to give way, and it was evident that it was not pleased with all the commotion Puffer was making.

By now, we were about four yards from the cat, stopped and waiting.

Being so close to such a fearless cat only added to Puffer's fury, and she was now lunging against the windshield. A chill penetrated my body as I heard the sealant beginning to crack as the dog repeatedly lunged at the glass. What had till now been a somewhat bemusing cat and dog situation now had the potential of becoming an immediate crisis.

It was a distinct possibility that my now unmanageable dog could push free the windshield. The thought became an instantaneous fear that this nervy cat would be joining us in the front seat of the Fiat . This was not good. I could not stop the dog, and I didn't want to hurt or kill the catamount. So I did the only thing left to do—I hit the horn.

Remember, this was a foreign car, or more precisely an Italian product with a most piercing, high-pitched twin Pareilli trumpet air horn.

Blarrrttttt, brassssttttt, the merged sounds shrieked across the snow.

At this point, I wish to observe, mountain lion or tabby, house or puddy . . . a cat is a cat.

Instantly, this several hundred pound beast leaped straight up, more than three feet in the air, and disappeared to the right into the snow filled dark of night. Scratch one feline menace.

Surprised by the sound of the horn, my dog momentarily sat back in stunned calm.

A pin-drop silence filled the car, save for the muffled hum of the engine and the heater fan momentarily. Needless to say, Puffer spent the next few minutes barking at the rear windscreen as we proceeded along the idyllic, crystal white paradise toward the lodge for a good nights unwinding.

The rest of the trip went without incident, although there was that reoccurring contemplation: What would have happened if the cat had attacked, or if the dog had popped out the windshield, or if the horn had not worked?

Best not go there.

But I will always remember the lesson, no matter the size . . . a cat is truly a cat.

Java, the Path Is Long

We Indians drink a lot of coffee. Just a fact. A habit I presume started with our trading with our South American cousins. Who knows?

Whatever, we do drink a lot of coffee. While downing another cup of joe, I thought of the dark brew's journey to that cup and penned the following.

Drip . . . drip . . . drip . . . trickle . . . flow . . .
gush in steam,
vapors of mountains and streams,
in jungle green, in rich verdant.

Long journey from hand picked,
to burlap on backs.
Spread and sorted,
grade dependent on color and nose . . .
again in burlap, or paper.

Trucks . . . crate and box . . .
ship dark and stifle . . .
bobbing on waves of green,
docked at last, a port strange to the homeland.

Trucks once more.

To shop and store.

Ground at last in cup or glass,

our nirvana achieved.

A cup of java, essence of our breeze.

I'm Too Old

In remembrance of the most remarkable man I have ever known—Jesse Stewart Barber, my grandfather.

Nearly all Native Americans today are of mixed blood. I would be inconsistent in paying respect to my ancestors if I did not pay tribute to the other tribes in my life, that of the Celts and Britons.

My mother's dad was a living example of virtue who neither cursed nor hated. He believed in the ethic of devotion to God, hard work, family love, and enjoing life. If he had a vice, it was smoking. He smoked his pipe. He even gave me my first Dr. Graybow and taught me how to enjoy the "pleasures of the leaf."

"Never inhale," he admonished, "that'll make you sick and just may give you the cancer." I never did inhale.

Well, truth be known, Grandpa Barber did have another vice. He loved with a devotion, the Cincinnati Reds baseball team. If it were possible, he would never miss a broadcast of the Reds on radio, and later TV.

Yep, he was as near a complete human as I have ever known. This is just one story about this incredible man.

To be yet young at 60, 70 or 80 is much preferred to being forty years old with those requisite black trimmed "over the hill" parties.

"You youngsters go out and play ball. I'm too old for that!" Haven't we all heard something like this at times from our elders?

"That is for young people," they would say. Or, "No thanks, I can't learn to do that. I'm just too darnedold to change."

People, as they get past their prime and of an age that is generally considered to be "old," start believing this silly mantra. Soon they find that because they are old, they have convinced themselves that they can no longer do that of which they are actually capable.

I find all this incredible.

All their lives they have been able to do as they pleased, anything they wanted. They were pretty much in control of themselves—maybe not as good as when they were twenty, but still able to do most everything they set their mind on doing.

However, there comes a point in everyone's life where they wake up and say, "I'm too old to do that anymore."

"I'm too old to ride a bike."

"Too old to swim."

"Too old to run."

"Too old to laugh with abandonment at things I used to enjoy."

"I'm too old to enjoy life, so I am just going to sit back and let it pass by me, blah, blah, blah."

With those thoughts in mind, I want to share with you a story that happened some years ago.

When the following event occurred, my grandfather Jesse Barber was well into his eighties. Grandpa Barber was an independent mix of hickory and fire, tied up with baling wire. Slight of build but with ample muscles, he was country tough. Although a farmer born to the earth, at times throughout his long life he had to make do with other jobs to make it all come together. I am blessed to have great and wonderful grandparents. They are my root stock.

He always had a smile, he was always happy. It was his way of sharing and giving and participating in life. I never recalled a time when he wasn't "doing something." He was always plowing, seeding, weeding, building, digging, or any other of a wide variety of activities that required his attention around his rural home and farm. Much of his life, he worked days in the factory and evenings and weekends on the land.

In the winter, he would tend to things indoors. He would do repairs around the house that he had "put off" during the summer. He was a cobbler by trade and during the cold weather, he would repair shoes for the family. Winter was time for papering the walls and sorting collections of this and that which seemed to just appear each year. There were icy walks and coal to bring in, clinkers and waste to be removed, trash to burn.

Living in the country meant always being busy. My grandpa did all this with never a complaint. They were the things that he had been taught to expect and care for. He did all this with a dignity rarely found in his time, and seldom found today. Jesse Barber was what you might call a working class country gentleman.

Each day was special to him. Each month meant something new and different to experience, but spring and summer were his special times. This was when he could enjoy his greatest passion, baseball.

As a young man he had played a bit at semi-pro with the Selby team, but he always kept his hand in the game. On Sunday afternoons, he could be found in a pasture "tossin' a ball" with the local guys. Throughout his life, his greatest pleasure was baseball, whether it be playing the game or turning on the radio to catch the Cincinnati Reds as the "boys of summer" plied their trade.

This was the man I have always held as my ideal for manhood.

On one occasion, I went to visit my grandfather to check on his supplies and to see if there was any work that he needed to have done. He lived up a "holler" in a small home perched in the hardwood forest hillside of rural southern Ohio.

As I drove up his lane from the gravel road below, I noticed that the front door to his home was open. Grandpa did that a lot. He was known not to close or lock his door for weeks at a time in good weather.

"People take care of each other up the holler," he would say. "It is a safe place to be." A place a lot of us wish the world would be like today.

I pulled my truck to a stop alongside the shed and walked up the steps to the house.

"Hey, Grandpa, you in there?" I called out.

"It's Jimmy, Grandpa. I came to visit," I continued as I opened the screen door and walked into the living room.

"Grandpa?" I queried.

As I glanced about the room, I saw his working pipe was sitting beside his smoking pipe on the tobacco stand. He had a pipe for pleasure and one for working, one that could take abuse. It was a bit unusual that both pipes were there on the stand.

Looking over the half wall into the kitchen, I could see the coffeepot on the stove with steam still rising from the spout. I knew it hadn't been long since it had been brewed.

I continued to look about for him. I went to his bedroom then looked in the bathroom. He wasn't to be found.

"Where the heck is he hiding?" I mumbled.

Finally, I walked out the back door onto the porch. It was empty. Beyond his backyard was the outdoor privy. The door with the hand-painted little half-moon stood ajar. I could see he wasn't in there either.

This was beginning to become a bit strange.

I tried calling again. "Grandpa, grandpa, where are you?"

Crash! Snap! Kerthud!

In the distance I heard the definitive sound of a limb falling. It wasn't like it had just dropped from a tree. By the sound, it had fallen through the leaves and branches from high up in the forest canopy.

Then I heard the sound of a saw—you know, the noise a handsaw reverberation makes as it is pushed and pulled back and forth.

Shish, shish.

As I walked up the path, I noticed that laying along the trail was some wiring. As I got to a small clearing, there was a whole bunch of small tree limbs laying by a tall hickory tree.

I looked up this now nearly de-nuded hickory tree and saw my grandfather perched at its top.

Now my granddad wasn't in his fifties, he was in his eighties at this time—too old to be climbing trees, one would say.

I looked up at him and said, "Grandpa, what in the world are you doing up there?"

He looked down and said, "Be with you in a minute, grandson."

I watched as he fastened a big fancy TV antenna to the top of the tree that he had hauled up on a rope. Then he fastened the wires to it and turned the whole rig in the general direction of Cincinnati and the television station that broadcasts the Reds' games.

I watched with great apprehension as this wirey, rickety old man climbed down the tree, one limb at a time. When he got to the bottom, he was a bit winded.

As he was getting his breath back, I asked, "Grandpa, are you okay?"

"Just fine, grandson," he smiled. "Let's go get some coffee."

While we were walking down the trail, I asked, "Grandpa, what in the world possessed you to strip that tree and put that TV antenna in its topnotch? You could have asked anyone in the family, and we would have been happy to do it for you."

He stopped and turned to face me. His eyes sparkled as he looked at me and said, "You know there is a big game on today."

He started to turn back downhill then paused. "I realized a while ago that I had gotten to the point where I put off things I should be doing, just 'cause I thought I was too old."

Stepping over a log, we continued down the path.

"Wasn't a week ago that I realized I'm not too old . . . unless I just can't do the work. So rather than ask for help, I gave'er a try," he stated. "I needed to find out for myself whether I was really too old."

"Well, sir, grandson, the proof is in the pudding. The antenna is up."

Opening the gate, we walked toward the back door.

"Let's fire up the ol' boob tube and see if we can catch that Reds game . . . they're playing dem bums, the Dodgers," he chuckled.

So we sat down and had our coffee, talked about this and that, and snapped some beans while we watched the game and smoked a pipe together.

The Reds took it from them once again . . . this time on Grandpa's TV rather than on the radio.

It was indeed a good day to be alive, and neither of us was "too old" to enjoy that day.

I gave up recreational smoking some years ago, and now only smoke a ceremonial pipe, except at times when miss my Grandpa Barber. Then I get out the Graybow he gave me, light up a bowl, and remember the day when I learned that I will never be "too old."

Cold Winter

Adapted from an anonymous work.

Native American society is replete with jokes about near everything. We get great joy in laughing, and I would be remiss if I didn't include at least one of the thousands of "Indian" jokes that have circulated for so many years. I recall my dad, Chief Ten Moons, telling this one when I was still a kid at home. It has been a staple of the Native American stand-up comics. Yet, as much as it is a joke, it is also another example of our using life as a learning tool. Let us discover the relationships within the Circle we call life.

It was one of those drop dead beautiful fall days down on the Potomac, a few miles outside the Capitol Beltway. The leaves were in riot color and the air was crisp with the beckon of winter. A small enclave of Delaware Indians who lived in the area asked their newly-elected Chief if the winter was going to be cold or mild.

The Chief knew he had to give an answer, but since he was a Chief living in a small modern Indian community near the center of the United States government, far from the rural areas to the west, he was not prepared to reply. If only there had been an Elder who had lived from the land and knew of its secrets to teach him, but they had long since passed away.

He was on his own. His first big executive decision was at hand.

The Chief closed his eyes in a contemplative manner and when he opened them, he looked to the sky and studied the clouds.

Try as he may, he couldn't tell what the weather was going to be. Wanting to make a good impression on his People, and to be on the

> **We are never more at risk to play the fool than when we are positive of our facts.**

safe side, he told them with great authority in his voice that the winter was going to be a cold one, and that they should collect wood so as to be prepared.

So all the Indians set about collecting wood so they'd be ready. But after a few days, being concerned that he may have misled his People and wanting to be a responsible leader, the Chief called the National Weather Service, asking, "Is the winter going to be cold this year?"

"It looks like this winter is going to be a cold one," the meteorologist replied.

This information sounded ominous, so the Chief went back to his tribe and told them to collect even more fuel in order to be prepared.

A week later, he called the meteorologist again. "Are you sure it's going to be a real cold winter?"

"Yes," the man replied, "it's without doubt going to be a very cold winter."

Again the Chief gathered the People and urged them to collect every scrap of wood they could find.

A couple of weeks later, he called the meteorologist again. "Are you absolutely, positively sure that this winter is going to be real cold?"

"No question," the man replied. "It's going to be one of the coldest winters on record."

Puzzled as to the certainty of the meteorologist, the Chief asked, "How can you be so sure?"

The weatherman replied, "The Indians are collecting wood like crazy."

7 Wisdom, and Other Elder Traits

We're the first people here.

We live here with the permission of the Great Spirit.

Thomas Banyacya, Hopi Elder
From *Through Indian Eyes*

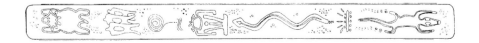

A Letter To My Grandchild

It is our tradition that on the occasion of a child in the family becoming an adult, it is the obligation of a grandparent, aunt, or uncle to spend time with the child-become-adult to offer last thoughts for the future. This is one such letter to my grandchild.

Dear Grandchild,

I want to share some thoughts with you that I have carried for a very long time now. Read this and then put it away for a while. On important occasions, or times when you feel the need, reread these thoughts, knowing that for all the days of your life I have loved you as my first Grandchild, my friend, and my answered dream-prayer from God. We both are aware that there is no blood connection between us. That makes the connection we have so much more important. You are my Grandchild in all ways. I will be your Grandfather all the days of my life.

In the tradition of the Shawnee-Mide', it is the responsibility of the Grandfather to share with his Grandchild the following truths.

Enjoy this time of your youth as if it were the most important time of your life. It truly is. Now are the days when you focus your vision upon the future, your goals and desires, for all the rest of your days. You will have a long time to accomplish your desires. Don't rush. Make the most of each day. Live each day as fully as you possibly can. Waste none of it. It is your gift from the Good Creator.

Society has decreed that you are now an adult, with all the rights and responsibilities that entails. However, neither society nor any person can tell you when you must give up being young. Grandchild, you know me well enough to know that I have never completely given up my youth. My thoughts and desires and visions are much the same as when I was your age. I remember as if it were yesterday my wanting to share my gifts, to create fine works of art, to write meaningful tomes, to make song and bring laughter into rooms to deadly serious, And today I still do these things.

Do not give up your right to grow as you see fit. This is your life, not mine or any other person's. This is your golden gift from God Himself, to be enjoyed and explored and developed all the long days to come.

Set goals to achieve. Envision dreams you want to become reality. Fill your waking hours with the most positive attributes possible, and allow no time for anything negative to have a part of your time. You only have a finite time allotted. Try not to waste it with negative emotions, hatred, envy, and vindictiveness. These are the ways of people who cannot control their destiny. You are above that. You can be your "dreamed self," if only you believe you can.

My Parents and Grandparents often reminded me of this simple truth . . . "that I could be and do anything I wanted . . . that I could never be stopped if I only tried hard enough . . . " Today I am respected, loved and looked up to. Today I am an inspiration to those who hear and see what I have become. Today I am successful in all the areas that I only dreamed of as a youth. Today I am at peace and am happy in all my days. These things you too can have, if you dream of them . . . and then set about achieving them.

> The door between the sanctuary of youth and the opportunity to bring life to that fow which we have so long trained opens wide but once. We must be ready to proceed at that moment's notice.

Grandchild, I have always believed that someday you would become a wise and important man who would inspire others to achieve their greatness. This I know will come about for I have dreamed this, this I have envisioned.

Things do not just happen though. You must be an active part in this process. Do important things. Give of yourself and your possessions. Each gift you give without reservation will return to you tenfold in ways you cannot imagine. Lead. Be compassionate. Show others an easier path, a better way. Speak always from the warmth of your heart. Fill your memories with your good works and loved people and enjoyed times. Fill your lonely times with those memories.

Allow no one to control your destiny. Permit no person or group or religion to direct your walk of life, your path to God. But speak with Him often and heed His directions. Give thanks often for all you achieve and ask not for yourself. Trust that others will be interceding on your behalf. They will. God will provide you with all you need to become the man He envisioned when He first thought of you and you became the child of His vision. We humans will inevitably let you down, but He will always guide your way. You only need to speak and listen.

My gift to you at this eighteenth year mark of your life is to share the truth given me so long ago:

"You can be all that you wish to be. No one can stop you. You will be a light for others to follow, if it is your wish."

Visit with me as time allows, in person, on the phone, or write me. Share your dreams and visions. Tell me of your accomplishments, and above all . . . enjoy!

Your devoted grandfather . . .

I Am In Balance

We are told that it is our responsibility to live in balance with all Creator's universe. We hold this to be a principle of great importance. It is our job. When I feel a loss of that balance, I return to these thoughts to refresh my recall of this task.

When I envision myself in my perfect balance, as I once was when He Who Creates With Thought first envisioned me, I was created in balance.

And like the old ones taught me, I am the sun-warmed Grandmother's child by day and am in Grandfather's calm, snuggled sleep at night. My life must reflect that balance.

I am the weightless maple seed of old as I gently circle to my Grandmother Tula to begin anew. I can and want to cause good for all the People, and know that I can see all our tomorrows in a vision set crystal clear. I am in complete, innocent harmony, filled with honor and dignity, and I am in my place of perfect balance. All my todays must be in balance.

I am the sum of all this and more when I am in my perfect balance. When I am not, I am lost and falling in the endless and overturned landscape created by the broken faith in my own balanced existence, and I endeavor once more to find the place of my perfect sacred balance.

That is the single reason I am here—it is my obligation to all the People. I am that upon which all the People past, and yet to come are balanced.

In This Ancient Place

Born near the site of historic Black Hoof's Old Town, in the occupied lands of the Shawandasse in the Ohio River Valley—on the sacred Mother Earth where my Grandfathers and Grandmothers are a part of the land—it is here, in this ancient place, I feel that I "know" this Ohio . . . it is my home.

Like my Shawnee and Fort Ancient ancestors, we have acknowledged our oneness with this ancient homeland. I feel the land, as if she were my physical Grandmother, and I am filled with the need to heal and comfort her from the abuses she has long endured. It is our source of life's renewal.

As I walk the Red Road, it is with the knowledge that it is not just for Shawandasse but for All My Relations. Therefore, I am dedicated to the reunification of all the Red People and demand the rightful honor and respect, that has so long been taken, be restored.

I invite all to join in the restoration of our beloved liberties to all our People. Lend your name, share your ideas, roll up your sleeves, or help raise funds. Pray. Argue your beliefs. Share your opinions but please, don't be indifferent.

We need the strength of your individual fiber, combined with the fibers of all concerned, to make a cord strong enough to mend this tear of twenty-five generations . . . the inherited self-deceit that is

> This is the sacred Mother Earth, the Holy Land where my parents and grandparents gave their measurement to this Place.

the prime source of the eventual annihilation of our "Nation of many Nations".

If a society cannot resolve the wrongs caused by its creation, it can never possess real honor and integrity. Despite proclamations and protestations, a nation bereft of these most basic qualities cannot prevail as a truly free society.

SWEETGRASS
PRAYER STICK
with TOURQUOIS

Dinner With . . .

Recently, I was challenged to "name three people who, if you could, you would want to have dinner with, and what would you ask them?" This caused me to ponder: "If it were possible, with whom would I like to have this opportunity? I came up with my three subjects, the three people who have most inspired me.

The first two are my father, Chief Ten Moons, and my mother, Nell. I am forever indebted to them for the gift of reassurance that there is nothing that I cannot achieve. My youth was shaped in a caring family who were at times dirt-poor, living in the rural Appalachia region of Ohio. No adversity has deterred the children of my parents. We have each, in our own way, achieved a level of distinction commiserate with our efforts. None of my siblings are failures. We are well educated, fully engaged in societal ministrations and authorities in our chosen fields.

My question would be, "Considering all my achievements and failures, have I attained that measure you envisioned when you first met me at my birth?"

The third person would be the Shawnee Shaman, Penageshe (1796-1803). He was a Bear Walker, a Shape-Shifter. He was one of the last "Speakers" who knew all practices and language of our originality passed down from the Ancient Ones. Even though we have lost three-fourths of our language (and there are only a few dozen who speak it), and because we only practice the major Ceremonies of past times, have we also

> There is no question more important than one that cannot be answered.

lost the center of our heritage, our spirituality?

In this light, my question to him would be, "In the pragmatism of your gifted vision, are we acceptable in this regressive childlike state?"

As you see, I most want to know that the wizened ones who have lived before me approve of what I have become. Their approval, confirmed or imagined, reflects the very basis of the value system of my People. We are taught that "all things are connected." We are taught that we are to "never dishonor the honored," that we are to "never disrespect the respectful." that we must "understand how the next seven generations and the past seven generations will be affected by our decisions," and that we "must never let the People die."

(This refers to the story of the Unbroken Cord from our Origination.)

My Life is a Mess

How many times have you observed someone and said, "Boy, that person's life is a mess." Or, "How can he live that way?" Equally important, you overhear others saying, "My life is so messed up!" At times, we even look at ourselves and acknowledge that, "This life I am living is a total mess." What to do?

Most of the mess we live in is that which we create. How can that be? We are so influenced by that which is outside our control. You say you don't have real choices, in jobs, what you get paid, and often even the opportunity for a good education. You take the best you can, but a lot of the time that is not enough. The kids get sick, or a hurricane or tornado strikes, or an earthquake damages your home. All these are the messes "just happen", you have little to no control over them. Yes, all this does occur. Mess happens. However, in truth, the vast majority of our "messes" come from within, from our lack of self-control.

It is the old story of the Pot and the Stick. The Blue Creek/Shawnee are taught that when we are born we are born, as a clay vessel with a long stick in it. Into this vessel or pot is placed all that happens to us, the good, bad, indifferent—everything that happens in and around us goes into this pot. And the stick? Well, it stands tall, above the pot's rim, so you can grab it and stir. But remember, it reaches all the way to the bottom.

Stirring this pot is like cooking where you stir the pot regularly to blend the flavors well. But if you get distracted—walk away to do the dishes, shuck the corn, whatever the chore—when you return the soup has burned the goodies on the bottom. Now you have a choice to make. You can empty out the food into another pot and continue, or

We control or are controlled, there is no middle ground. Your decision to manage your life empowers your destiny.

you can simply not put your spoon down to the bottom. That way you won't scrape up the burnt stuff. The soup will taste good as long as you do not disturb the bad stuff at the bottom.

Well, life is a lot like that. The good things float at the top, and the bad things sink and gum up on the bottom. It seems we try to put as much distance as we can between us and the bad things. But with life's pot, we too often take our stick, when we are frustrated or not paying attention, and reach far down and stir up that junk at the bottom again. Those bad things float right back to the top and before long, we are reliving them over and over again. The more we relive them, the more frustrated we get, then the more we stir the pot, and the more we dig at the bottom—it is a never-ending cycle.

An elder once told me, "As you fill your Pot of Life, the badness, all those things you don't want to relive, sink quickly to the bottom. As soon as things settle, insert your stir-stick down into the pot until it just touches the top of all that muck. When it reaches the sludge, break off the top so that it can no longer reach into the mess at the bottom. Continue to do this throughout your whole life. When you get to the end of your journey, when the vessel is full, you will find your stick is much shorter. You will also find that you have lived a long life without reliving all that trash, that badness, and thus not bringing it back into you life continually.

"By living only in the goodness at the top of your pot, you have been able to enhance your life and that of those around you. Yes, you know the muck is still there. Never forget the past, they are the lessons learned. Know, and accept that you have wasted that part of your life, but also know that you have been able to enjoy the richness of your life, because you continued to shortened your stick along the way. This story has stood me well—I hope it does with you."

HOPI TAAWAKATSINA
SUN KATSINA DOLL
LATE 19TH C

Why Are There Masks?

In the time before the New Ones had come, even before the Animal People, the Great Master of Life envisioned the souls of all that were yet to be thought of . . . and these visions became the Spirits of the People. In this time, they inhabited all and were to be the conservators of Tula, the earth, as we know it.

When the Creator conceived an image of Tula, it instantly became real, for Creator made all things with Its Thought. Starting with the First Parents, and those of the Leafed People, the furred and the winged ones, and those who crawled and swam, and lastly the two-leggeds, The Master thought of each in turn and, therefore, they were. Then He caused the Spirits of the People to separate into Living People and Spirits. The Living People became the New Ones, they became the People of Tula. The Spirit that they had come from now became their guides, their Spirit Guides.

They lived together in this magnificent place that had been envisioned. In all things, the Spirit Guides assisted the newly created as needed, and they all walked their paths in harmony and balance.

There was only one law—live in balance . . . with each other.

As long as the law was kept, the New Ones and their Spirit Guides lived in peace and dignity. Everything had its place and purpose.

This was as it should be and life was wonderful. This was the way of life for a very long time until one day, one of the New Ones became angry and spoke ill of another. He told untruths and spoke of evils the person had never committed. This caused a great hurt; and in this imbalance, the law had been broken.

The punishment was that all the New Ones and their children's children would never be able to see their Spirit Guides again. The New People were most lonely and longed to view the magnificence of their friends, the Spirits.

> Fear has no place with understanding.

At last, Creator compromised and gave honor and responsibility to those two-leggeds, called the True Seers and their descendants—who, by exemplary belief, had achieved a proper spiritual balance—to make the effigy masks and dance the path of the Spirit Guides.

On occasion, these descendents are chosen by the Spirit Guides to show us their images, in order that the New Ones may once again be properly guided. They are our conduit, our connection between the New Ones and the Spirit People.

All this was told to the Mide' Sachems of the People "Who Move the Earth."

Today one of those True Seers, Wasian, the Shawandasse mask maker continues this tradition. She is an ancient soul steeped in the spiritual traditions of her ancestors. Since her early childhood, she has been connected, bound to her beloved Grandmother Earth, a single spirit removed in great part from her peers.

As she constructs these masks, she uses the gifts provided. Her feathers have fallen from the sky and bone lay sun-bleached upon the earth . . . leather, skin, and quill from the path of life's circle given. Each is filled with the spiritual essences of its origin and are collected or gifted to her. Each is given that we may see our Guides. It is in this manner of service that Wasian has found the meaning for her existence.

She has no choice in the matter. She has been chosen to create these images from the shadowed memory of her First Parents. From those who have lived on her ordered-path, her parents, and theirs before them, and those through all ages, she is guided to see and make these magnificent effigy masks. Just as today's Spirit Dancers of the many

First Peoples who live on the Great Turtle Island show the Spirit Dance Path, Wasian shows their likeness.

This modern woman does not acknowledge or claim any special abilities or powers. This is simply her path. Yet, she has been widely acknowledged for her unique connection to the Ancient Ones. And the observations by many indigenous Spiritualists and Elders confirm the significance of her distinct True Seer obligations.

Wasian allows us to see our Spirit Guides. This is as it should be.

Adean.

The Lesson of the Electric Mower

Native Americans in the rural southern Ohio area of Appalachia are always "making do" with the equipment at hand. Why spend good money to replace what can be repaired? This story is about my father's stubbornness over a device that could possibly have been the making of my demise.

When I was a kid, our dad bought a used electric lawn mower. You know, the ones with a real long cord that was forever trying to get wrapped up onto the spinning blade. Dad was careful to teach us how to mow in a pattern that would keep us from backing over the cord. But I was a kid. Who listened at that age? I was forever catching the cord in the blades (and repairing the same)!

We lived in the small country town of Buena Vista, Ohio. The town was know for its large property lots, and ours was no exception. The area of town that we lived in was divided into lots about 75-feet wide by 200-feet deep, which provided a decent place for a garden behind the house and a nice front and side yard of grass. My parents spent what they could to improve the place, and it looked real nice.

Keeping it that way was a constant chore. We had been using a push mower, but Dad had run across this mower and bought it for a good price. He always "bought at a good price."

The biggest drawback of an electric mower was that the cord that feds the powers from the house or barn seemed to always hide in the wrong place. Electric mowers needed little less that an awaiting outlet in which to be plugged. Connected to its source, it was ready to spin away the tall grass. Sure, there is a lot less maintenance than a gas mower, but there was always "the cord." You see, the blade was indiscriminate in doing its job. It cut the grass just fine, and if you were not careful, the cord equally as well.

When I went out to mow, it soon became the custom to would grab a roll of "friction tape." You know, the type made of cloth and a tar-like substance. Just the thought of friction tape sends OSHA into a frenzy.

As I unwound the cord from the handle to plug it into the wall socket, I would inspect it for cuts and nicks. Each damaged part was carefully taped to cover the bare copper wire that carried the current. This was an important part of the ritual of mowing—repairing the cord before you plugged it in . . . or else, WHAM!

The instant a bare wire section of the cord got grounded, the electrical current would hit you like lightning and make you shake like you had a high fever until you could let go of the mower.

Oh, how I hated to mow on a wet day! Just as soon as the cord got wet up to the frame, B-r-r-r-t . . . WHAM! it would hit.

The first time it happened each mowing day was always the worst.

I carried a dry rag with me to keep that last foot or two, next to the mower, bone dry. Worked most of the time, but when I got careless . . . oh, my, did I pay for my laziness!

Electricity and its uses were not a new concept in the city; but in the country, we were still learning about its wonders, and dangers. It had been just a few years before that my dad had been instrumental in forming the first Rural Electric Cooperative in our area. Even though our home and barn were wired and we had several electric appliances, I believe that it was much later that he became fully aware of its more deadly attributes.

For the longest time, while I was mowing that summer, there was the nagging thought that "my dad was trying to kill me." I found out later that he had never known that I was being shocked. He was mortified when I first told him that, as a kid, I had been getting shocked by the electric lawn mower. He had never thought about my being in danger from the mower. It was a guilt that I believe he carried to his grave.

Looking back on it all, I realize that Dad was most protective of my well being. Sure, he would warn me of, say, the fire in the stove, but he knew that I would have to touch it to learn the lesson. He was always there at those times to make sure I didn't get hurt too badly. It was the way the parents of that day helped us learn the difference between real dangers and those imagined.

The electric mower was one of my self-enlightening moments.

As the summer progressed, I slowly realized that I had learned a healthy respect for electricity and what it could do. After that I was most careful to repair and maintain electrical equipment.

Lessons like that were never forgotten.

Although I am most careful around electricity today, I can still taste the electricity in my mouth after having received a shock. The taste was akin to when you touch a battery with your tongue to test it, just a lot stronger.

In the time when our ancestors lived with the Animal People, our young people were taught to learn by experience. This doesn't mean that the children were unnecessarily exposed to danger, but it was important that they learned quickly what would hurt them. They were educated at the old "school of hard knocks." Today we strive to protect ourselves and our children from the most minute exposure to any danger or discomfort. We are obsessed over germs and unseen evils and whatever our minds can conjure up to cause us to be afraid. There is enough in reality that we must bear. I do not understand the need to wallow in these other "possible" fears. No wonder so many people today are seeing a therapist.

It seems a pity.

Who is going to teach them how to protect their children?

The Tree and the Eagle

In the time before our Grandfathers and Grandmothers, after He Who Creates with His Mind had caused all the Plant People to exist, He noticed that some of the new People were continually trying to reach higher in the sky . . . trying to touch His Face. These were named the M'tekyah . . . the Tree People. They tirelessly continued to get closer. By this dedicated act, they became the tallest of all the Green People.

Once, when Creator was thinking about their passion, He envisioned them breaking free of Grandmother Turtle's back, flying to be in his presence. Immediately this became reality.

The Tree People did not have to fly from Grandmother's back. A new Ppeople had been created. They were called the M'tekwaw—the Eagle People—and they made the topmost branches of the Tree People the place for their lodge.

The connectedness between the Tree and the Eagle teaches that if you try with all your ability to succeed, Creator will help you achieve your goals (a Shawnee Creation story).

No one can exist as an island, relationships are required for success.

The Shawnee, as all Native Americans, are well known as the first environmentalists. As our ancient stories tell, we have always held the Tree People in the greatest respect. They are our Elders and are a vital part of our balance. They teach a good, positive lesson to our People about devotion to cause.

The Old Stone Pipe

The old red stone pipe felt as the hawk's tail feather,
ever lighter as each of my brothers and sisters
returned it to my care.

The sacred leaves made smoke that carried our prayers,
our very thoughts, to Creator as we each, in turn,
fulfilled our ancient obligation.

So many times, hands creased old . . . hands smooth
with youth . . . hands of our grandfathers and grandmothers who had held the old red stone pipe.

The painful salt tears of the holy men gone before now,
had stained their weathered cheeks as they guided
their People in the smoke prayer.

Desire was always strong, but the hope of many had
dimmed as the generations of Shawandasse had been
herded to many strange places.
The prayers came first as the rapids of spay-le-wah-
seppe, then darkness of the passing years dimmed the
vision - at last the Bundle Fire was dark.

For a time, the old red pipe laid cold, in darkness.
Then the dream again had been the fire's rekindling,
once again we made the smoke prayer.

Once again a Shawandasse Kitch Okema, a great chief
called Tukemas, (Hawk at the setting sun) had
breathed life to the sacred fires.

The Bundle of the People of the South Wind once again
lay on Grandmother's breast and in Grandfather's
view. The circle was again complete.

Now this was not as were the days of the ancient ones.
This time the pipe ceremony was different.
This time we were no longer praying for the return.

No longer did we have to pray for the day when we,
the South Wind People, would be able to have a place,
a place to call Shawnadasse.

All the prayers of all the hands and lips that have
touched this old red pipe have come to life,
as now we have the returned land.

Now the People of the South Wind have the returned
land. After so many lifetimes of the ancient ones, we
now can call a piece of soil sacred.

Grandmother's breast will once again nurse her children. Grandfather's tears will now be those of joy upon the Shawandasse Returned Land.

This is the smoke prayer answered.

This is as it should be.

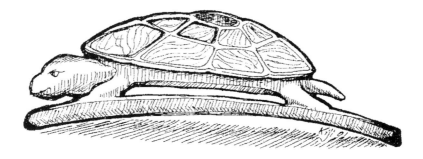

Will We Make a Difference?

In the telling of my View from the Medicine Lodge, *I have tried to keep an objective outlook as I relate the stories and thoughts. I know that there are "things to be attended" but I have tried to place them in the best light for understanding. In this essay, I want to speak plainly so that there will be no misunderstanding as to what I am saying. I believe that this openness is good for both you, the reader, and myself. Thank you for understanding.*

By the late 1880s, the Americans were finally able to conclude the continual war and invasion they had first begun over two hundred years prior as British Colonists. The American army had relentlessly chased us from our homelands, through winter cold and summer's searing heat (women and children included), until at last, under the direct orders of the President of the United States, they had finally destroyed the armies of the "Indian Patriots."

"Indians" indeed! Because of a lost Italian explorer and his search for a new route to India, we not only had been driven from the lands of our ancestors, but now we were striped of our real identities . . . Navajo, Dakota, Shawandasse, Kansans, Narragansett and hundreds of other names of Nations of People who were here to first welcome these misguided invaders.

During the years following their declaration of independence, this brash new Nation, on orders of their Presidents, used their army to systematically seize the sovereign lands of the Nations of Indigenous People. This was done under the guise of "treaties" to purchase Indian Lands, with the full knowledge that these people did not recognize title or deed. The land belonged to everyone, and no one had authority to sell it.

In a continual violation of basic law, and under these illegitimate treaties, the Government of the United States then apprehended and incarcerated the Citizens of these invaded Nations, eventually placing them in concentration camps and prisons west of the Mississippi River.

The relentless relocation and "aculturalization" were repeated over and over. Many of these war refugees, under the leadership of their wise elders, were able to retain and perform most of the important aspects of their Nation's past, and kept their traditions and ceremonies. For those who escaped capture and relocation, the years were filled with the fear of being found . . . they were considered fugitives of the United States Government, and a price for their capture was constant.

In the 1920s, the Congress of the United States imposed citizenship on all "Indians" residing within the boundaries of the then contiguous forty-eight states. By this act, we had become "Native Americans" with all the rights of any other citizen.

However, this unilateral act assumed that the People of the many Nations had relinquished their rights of citizenship of their Sovereign Nation. In many cases, they had not. As a historical note, equal rights have still not been afforded all Native Americans, and the "Indian Wars" continue, even to this date. This muddled

> When Creator made the Indian, He made us with the clay from our Grandmother's loving breast, and baked us in the warm smile of Grandfather Sky . . . and He threw in a good portion of scrap iron . . . needed to deal with the world today.
>
> Hopi Elder
> Riley Sunrise

relationship with the United States continues unresolved and many of the People today consider themselves "dual citizens."

For the most part, however, we are passionate supporters of this now great country. Most of our best warriors, men and women alike have fought, and many have died in the defense of the ideals of the United States. We are perhaps stronger "Americans" than most because we have *volunteered* again and again to fight for this "Sister Nation." the same Nation that nearly destroyed our very existence.

As we face the present, and all the tomorrows to come, it is with the knowledge that we have, can, and will make a difference. Because we have kept sacred the gifts of Tradition passed down by our Grandfathers, and their Grandfathers . . . we have honored them. By doing so, we have honored ourselves. Because we have followed their ways, we have preserved intact the Cord that connects us with the First Mother. We are at one with all our past.

With the honor and connectedness given by our ancestors, we now have the fibers needed to make "our basket," in which we will continue to store our gifts. As long as the cord is unbroken, we will continue to be.

Tomorrow will hold many surprises, both good and bad. We have long taken pride in the distinction that we prefer to make our own way. What we may lack in education and resources, we can more than make-up for with diligence and dignity.

To paraphrase the Hopi Elder, Riley Sunrise, "When Creator made the Indian, He made us with the clay from our Grandmother's loving breast and baked us in the warm smile of Grandfather Sky . . . and He threw in a good portion of scrap iron . . . needed to deal with the world today".

How right he is.

It is so important that we ALL understand the needs of today's Native People.

These needs are simple. We need . . .

. . . to be allowed to continue the Traditions of our Ancestors, to keep the Cord unbroken while being an important contributing unit of today's American community.

. . . to plan for the future of our children's children in a way that will ensure that their goals will be attainable in this same manner.

. . . to keep and honor our responsibilities to both our Ancestors and our Descendants, in equal balance . . . as Creator has always intended.

. . . to address and resolve the long ignored Treaties between the many "Indian" Nations and the United States, including the promised representation in Congress that these agreements have indicated, and to find the solution of our relationship with the United States Government . . . for the good of *all*.

The indigenous People and all other Americans need to trust in the Native Americans' abilities and our time-hardened determination to accomplish these . . . and other goals . . . as we have in the past.

Each of us needs you to invest in our future. By helping the American People understand the above, we will be investing in *our* future. Each word spoken, or every hour given to strengthen this understanding, will in turn, multiply many fold for the betterment of all the people today . . . and for the many generations not yet born.

Our efforts today will become a part of history.

We *can* make a difference.

The Life Circle We Call Earth

This is a Mide' story of our connectedness to all things. It teaches us the need to understand that everything we do has an effect on all others.

In the beginning, in the place of trees, the people of shadows and of mists, the first parents of all, came into the center of light and sky to form the great circle of life.

Then Spider Grandmother connected with her magic web each heart of first parents until they were all as one, united and in perfect balance.

Kiji Manito looked upon this web, declared it of greatest peace and beauty, and sat at the very center.

Again. Grandmother wove her web into Creator's heart and into all the first parents.

It was here and at this time that we became the Circle of Life, connected forever as we were to our mothers at time of first breath, in body and spirit, to all within the circle.

For as the life-cord that bound us to our mother made us a part of her, we are also a part of all of Creation's gifts—no better—or no less than all we resonate in good harmony or by bringing chaos into all the land . . . It is our choice.

It is our job to make of it as we may, a place better or crazed by each action and thought and deed as we cause to form by our very being, the Life Circle we call Earth.

Dare to Live the Proud Dream

Each instance and thought that returns us to the way of truth, the way of our Grandfathers, brings the Shawandasse nearer to the dream envisioned by the spirits that guide us. Without these precepts, we are not of the South Wind but only viewers on the edge of the Spirit Dance, watching as it passes by. Without living, exhibiting, and expressing our true heritage, we are the clay pot, empty and cold.

How does one say, "I am proud?" How will others know we are the leading edge of Tecumseh's lance, the next generation of Shawandasse? If we do not continually express in deed and word, "I am Shawandasse," we have failed.

My spirit soars each day knowing I am a Shawandasse Elene. I feel the spirit of my Grandfathers who fill me with their pride. Pride that one more day this modern Shawandasse will walk proudly and boldly forth to proclaim that we are still "A People." My mind is . . . my heart is . . . my image is . . . my spirit is of the South Wind.

Megwich Ni Kitch Okema Tukemas (My thanks to you my great Chief Hawk at the Setting Sun) for lighting the way through the forest of uncertainty and the darkness that the European tribes brought to this sacred land of the Turtle Island.

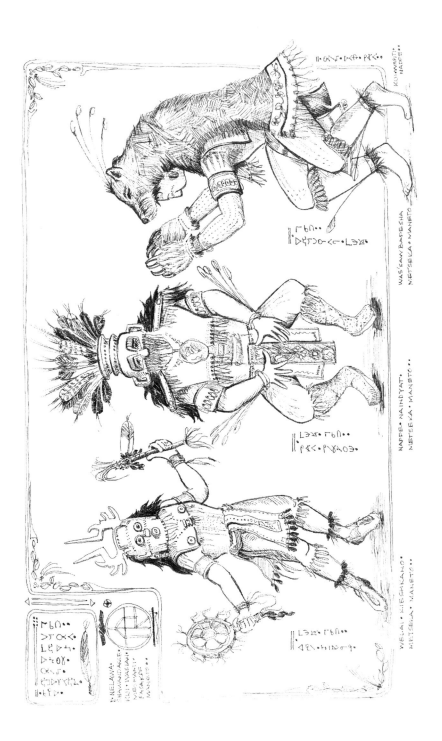

Mystical Spirits

Great Animal People, Mystical Medicine Spirits

We Dance the Spirit Dance Ceremony . . .

To celebrate and honor all things for they are also Creator's Brothers, we humble ourselves always before the Animal People because they were first, and we are but the last thought of Creator's Great Plan.

We Dance the Spirit Dance Ceremony . . .

We ask for their Life Gift because they must give of themselves, and that we have no right to choose their Life without their permission. We are of them, and they are of us. This is always as it should be.

Deer with Antlers Dancer Spirit . . .

A Ceremony Dance in respect and honor to the Deer People to ask their permission to send them through the veil that we may have food, clothing, and tools, as it should be.

Water Carrier Dancer Spirit . . .

A Ceremony Dance to thank Gicelamukaong, Kiji Manito, and Nanabusho for the gift of water and its Spirit that carries our Spirit in our bodies during this life, as it should be.

Frightening Bear Dancer Spirit . . .

A Ceremony Dance to honor and respect the Mighty Bear People to ask their permission to send them through the veil that we may have food, clothing, and tools, and to fear them for they are most powerful. This is always as it should be.

8   Appendix

Fry Bread

No book about the American Indian would be complete without a recipe for this staple. Try the one below. It is an easy-to-make mix and so tasty.

Fry Bread was first made by reservation Plains Indians using government supplies such as white flour, salt, and lard. They are not exactly wholesome by today's standards. They may have a little fat, cholesterol, and sugar here and there, but they are delicious.

Indian Fry Bread

2 cups flour (high gluten)
1 tsp. sugar
1/2 tsp. salt
1/2 tsp. baking powder
1 tbs. lard/Crisco/whatever
Approx. 1 cup water
Mix dry ingredients, add lard till crumbly. Add water until wet as possible and still workable. Knead till elastic. Break off tennis ball size chunks and work into patties like tortillas 1/2-inch thick. Then work, stretching like pizzas until 1/8-inch thick and a little roll on edges.
Fry at 375° until golden. Serves 2.

Out thanks to Grandmother, Amanda Toupin Martell Neddeau, a Pottawatomi, who left this recipe for others to enjoy.

Enjoy this recipe and know it is offered with love.

History of the
Shawnee Nation United Remnant Band

The Shawnee Nation United Remnant Band is NOT a federally recognized Indian tribe. Federally recognized Indian tribes have a treaty relationship with the United States government. Tecumseh DID NOT sign a treaty with the United State government.

The Shawnee Nation URB is a STATE-RECOGNIZED Tribe. This state recognition is NOT a token acknowledgement from a single senator or representative as commonly believed. It took two years of testimony hearings in front of a Special House Committee and legislation to be voted upon and passed by both the Senate and the House of Representatives. This Joint resolution was passed by the House of Representatives in July 1979 and the Senate on January 29, 1980. The Shawnee Nation URB is the only Ohio State-Recognized Indian tribe.

The Shawnee Nation URB does not receive any federal or state funding of any kind.

After Tecumseh's death in 1813, most of his warriors and their families decided to remain together as a Shawnee group. By the 1840s there were 36 Shawnee communities existing in Ohio, Indiana, Kentucky, West Virginia, Pennsylvania, and a few other states. Thick Water, who was Tecumseh's first cousin, best friend, first warrior, and personal bodyguard, became the "leader" of this Remnant Shawnee group. Tecumseh's children and other family members went to Oklahoma after Tecumseh's death. Most members of the Shawnee Nation URB are descendants of the remnant families who lived in the 36 Shawnee communities.

The Remnant Shawnee leadership continued through Thick Water's line for seven generations to today's date. Thick Water's name in

Shawnee is Paughp, which eventually became Pope. Hawk Pope, a direct descendant of Cornstalk (Tekonsha) and Thick Water, was elected "Chief" by his people in 1971 when he was 30 years old.

The Shawnee Nation, URB was reorganized in 1971 gathering the remaining Shawnee descendants from the 36 communities. At the time of reorganization, the Remnant Band had 312 people on its rolls. By 1995, the Shawnee Nation URB numbered over 600 members. After genealogical proof of at least 1/16 Shawnee blood and two full years of probationary time, the Shawnee Council takes a vote on whether or not to accept a petitioner into the Tribe. Meeting all requirements does not automatically guarantee full Tribal status.

In 1989, the Shawnee Nation, URB purchased their first twenty acres three miles southeast of Urbana, Ohio, in Champaign County. In the subsequent years that followed, more adjacent acreage was purchased. Shawandasse, the Ohio Shawnee Tribal Homeland, now totals 140 acres. It includes a 32'x100' Community Center, fully equipped with kitchen, two baths, and a Great Room complete with terracotta tile dance circle. Tribal Councils, ceremonies, and other Shawnee gatherings are held on this land. The Shawnee traditional ceremonies, songs, language, dances, crafts, and skills are kept alive through education and practice of Tribal members. These traditions have been passed down from generation to generation and continue today with our children.

In December of 1995, the Shawnee Nation URB purchased Zane Shawnee Caverns and Southwind Park. This family-oriented park hosts a 3/8 mile limestone cavern and includes over 65 campsites (RV and tent), 8 cabins, fishing, swimming, hiking, picnicking, and recreation areas. The park hosts an annual the Shawnee Woodland POWWOW. The Shawnee & Native Woodland Museum was added, which features Hopewell, Fort Ancient and Ancient to early historic Shawnee artifacts.

As of January 2000, the total acreage of Shawnee-owned land in Ohio totals 330 acres. This is the first Tribally-Owned Shawnee land in Ohio since 1830. One acre of this Ohio land was gifted to Chief Buck Captain for the Eastern Shawnee Nation.

The Shawnee Nation URB can be reached by writing to:

Shawnee Nation United Remnant Band
7092 State Route 540
Bellefontaine, Ohio 43311

History of the Blue Creek People— Eski'seppi Naube

The Blue Creek People, the ancestors of the Watters clan/family, have lived in Adams, Scioto, and Brown Counties since the earliest histories of that area. The Blue Creek People are a very private, long-serving sub- community made up of families from both the Raven and Scioto sects of southern Ohio. Our oral tradition tells us that we descend from the People who made the mounds and effigy earthen works along the Ohio River. We are now mostly known as Shawnee because of the alliance between the Talig'wah and the Shawnee that happened long ago.

In a time before the first Europeans came to our lands, there was a great devastation upon our People. The Shawandasse (People of the South Wind) had traveled into our homelands, found us in this sickly state, and cared for and healed our weak and afflicted—a bond that is honor bound, never to be discarded.

Many of our traditions have been influenced by that alliance, but we still retain much of our mound-builder ancient culture. An example is the Serpent Mound, one of the places that our People have held sacred. Some Shawnee feel this is a place of great evil, and indeed great evil has been perpetrated at this site. The Shawnee oral tradition tells them of Matchemanito, the evil serpent-deity who tries to destroy them. We Blue Creek People honor their tradition but are told that this was an ancient sacred home of our Snake Clan People. This place, along with Fort Ancient, Fort Hill, and the many other earthen edifices along the Ohio River, form the basis of our ancient traditions.

The predominant clan/families of the Talig'wah/Shawnee in the Blue Creek area are the Waters, White, Enyart, Price, Gilliland, Cooper, Lewis, Eastham, Easter, Perry, and Raider.

During the time of Tecumseh and Black Hoof, the Blue Creek People were a crucial part of the warrior force gathered to protect the homelands from the Americans. On October 5, 1813, our combined People were savagely defeated at the Battle of the Thames. Here the beloved War Chief Tecumseh was slain.

This was a devastating blow to the People, and most returned to their familial clan villages to await the inevitable. Some of the families reestablished their communities secluded deep in isolated woodland areas. The People from Raven Rock, Sinks, and Blue Creek went into the near inaccessible Appalachian hollows of Scioto and Adams Counties. Here they were protected from discovery by their long-time "white" friends who lived nearby. The Blue River, Bucks Town, and Big Sandy families did likewise.

These People gradually began assimilation. They assumed "American sounding" names and became a part of the fabric of the new American frontier. During this time, they kept the traditions and ceremonies as best they could. The Blue River People, today known as the Shawnee Nation United Remnant Band were probably the most successful in this endeavor. All Shawnee today, and those not yet born from the Earth, owe a tremendous debt to these brave Keepers of the Ancient Way.

The Blue Creek People recognized the need for unity among the clan/family communities that have survived the attempted destruction of the once mighty Talig'wah/Shawnee alliance. In 1979, the older children oined their father Chief Ten Moons and affiliated with the Blue River Community's Shawnee Nation URB. Within that tribal structure, Chief Ten Moons became a Tribal Elder. His eldest daughter, Tula Nappe, served as Buffalo Clan Mother for several years, and his middle son kiji wapiti nappe, represented the Eagle Clan for eight years before being elected the current Buffalo Clan Chief. In 1991 eldest son Kepish founded the Nishnas Chantoon (The People Speak) and is now an Elder on Council.

Tula Nappe has retired from active life with the URB and has concentrated her mother-love for the clan/families in the traditional Blue Creek People's homeland. She is the Principal Chief of the Shawnee Blue Creek Tribe.

Today's leaders are just five generations removed from the last sitting Chief of the Shawnee Lawalaway (John Perry), the Headman during the "Recovery Time" following 1813. From the final enactment of the Indian Removal Act (1832) to 1860, Thomas Waters held the clan/families together in the Adams County Blue Creek area. After the Civil War, many non-Indians moved into the tri-county area. It became important to further assimilate, so our family added a "t" to the name. The iron-fisted Headman "Pa" G.T. Watters (from 1860 to 1910) made the change and centered the clan over the hill, south of Blue Creek, near the mouth of Ohio Brush Creek. For over fifty years (1910 circa to 1964), his son Chief Big Dad Watters was Headman. He shared the leadership upriver a few miles at Sandy Springs with his wife Ma Jessie and the "Price Women." From 1964 until his death in 1993, Chief Ten Moons was the "Father" of the Blue Creek People.

For tens of centuries, our People have been centered within a thirty mile radius of our ancestral ceremonial village in the hills near the confluence of the Lower Twin Creek in Scioto county and Blue Creek in Adams County. Today our clan/family are scattered across the Great Turtle Island but still hold annual reunions at the lodge of Kepish Waters and his Shawnee/Lenapi wife, Ketiwa.

This information is my best recollection. It is founded in archival provenance and the oral histories as told to me by my father, Chief Ten Moons; my grandfather, Chief Big Dad; his son, George T. Watters; my great aunt, Jean Price; and other family elders of the Blue Creek and URB People. I am also forever indebted to Chief Hawk Pope and

the Elders and leaders of the Blue River families that are the Shawnee
Nation URB.

My mark and signature,

kiji wapiti nappe (Jim Great Elk Waters)

v-

-(

∞

—

|>

À

Maps

Map—Ohio Area

- - - Blue Creek Mide' Territory
..... Mound Builder Limit of Expansion

Map—Shawnee URB sites

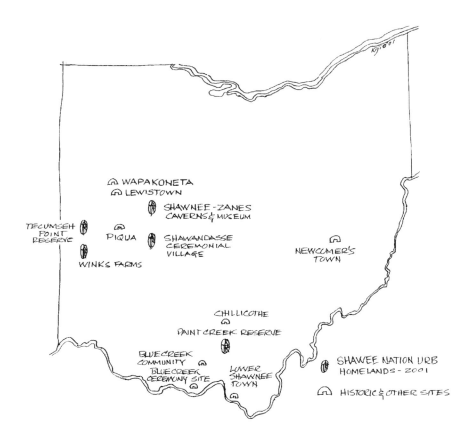

Map—Blue Creek

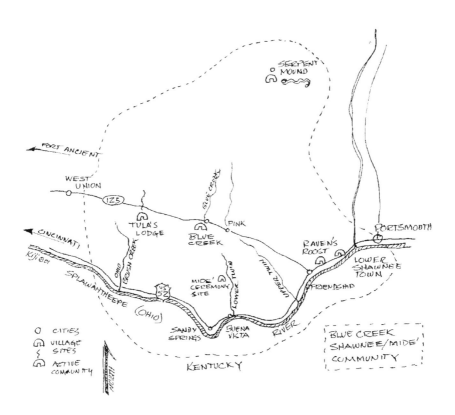

SERPENT MOUND

FORT ANCIENT

WEST UNION

125

CINCINNATI

Kijibou

SPLAWANTHEEPE (OHIO)

52

OHIO BRUSH CREEK

TULA'S LODGE

BLUE CREEK

BLUE CREEK

PINK

MIDE' CEREMONY SITE

LOWER TWIN

UPPER TWIN

RAVEN'S ROOST

PORTSMOUTH

LOWER SHAWNEE TOWN

FRIENDSHIP

SANDY SPRINGS

BUENA VISTA

RIVER

KENTUCKY

O   CITIES
     VILLAGE SITES
     ACTIVE COMMUNITY

BLUE CREEK SHAWNEE/MIDE' COMMUNITY

Map—Serpent Mound

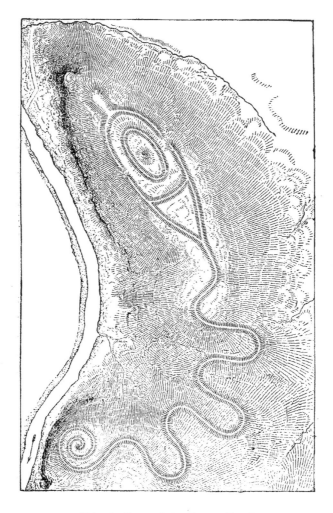

Holmes's Figure of the Serpent Mound.

Glossary

Disclaimer: All definitions are by the author or are from the *Cambridge International Dictionaries* and/or *Merriam-Webster Dictionary* unless otherwise indicated.

Mason, 32nd Degree: High ranking title of the Masonic Order of the Freemasons, member of a large, old and powerful secret society for men in which all the members help each other and use secret signs to communicate with each other.

aculturalization: to force a culture upon a people.

adean: (ah'dee ia in) Algonquian: It is ended.

akotha: *n* (ah'cootha) Algonquian: father.

All My Relations: From the Lakota metakuye oyasin (mah'tahk'we ae'seein) meaning literally we are all related.

Anishinaabe: *n.* (Ahnish'in aube *of the water* Algonquian-Wakasan) the Ojibwa People, their language

Apache: *n* (ahpach'ee:) American Spanish, perhaps from Zuni *a·*pacu Navajo, Apachean; 1745: a member of a group of American Indian peoples of the southwestern U.S.: any of the Athabascan languages of the Apache people.

Appalachia: *n* (A (as in cap) pah·la·chah) Apalachee Indian: a region in the E United States. A generally impoverished area of the southern Appalachian Mountains, the usually including NE Alabama, NW Georgia, NW South Carolina, E Tennessee, W Virginia, SE Ohio, E Kentucky, West Virginia, and SW Pennsylvania.

arbor: *n* (are'bor) 14th century Middle English *erber* plot of grass, arbor, from Middle French *herbier* plot of grass, from *herbe* herb, grass: a shelter of vines or branches or of latticework covered with shrubs used as a shelter for the Drum at powwow's

aya-angwa-a'mizin: (iyah eahn'gwah a'mzn – *to go carefully* Algonquian)

ayeia: *adv* (aeye'ya) Algonquian, used to express acceptance, willingness or agreement.

Azteca: *n* (ahzt ae ka Nahuatl language) the place of the cranes, of or relating to the Nahuatl people who established an empire in Mexico that inhabited the great plateau of that country whose civilization was at its height at the time it was overthrown by Cortes in Spanish conquest of 1519

Babackis'iganatuk:

Baha'i: *n* (baa-hi Persian, a follower of Bahaullah, *the Splendor of God*, from Arabic) of or relating to a world religion founded in 1863 in Persia based on Baha'u'llah's Baha'i (Prophet who was born in Persia in 1817 and died in 1892) revelation for kingdom of God and Peace on Earth, emphasizing the spiritual unity of all humankind, a teacher of or a believer in this faith.

Bear Walker: *n.* Shawnee, a Native American spiritual leader that is trained to invoke supernatural powers, able to transport oneself to other places by the use of the power of thought, a Shapeshifter.

birthing lodge: *n* Shawnee/Algonquian, a small round dome shaped building where women go to give birth. It is equipped with traditional birthing supplies for the occasion. Men are not allowed in the birthing lodge.

Black Hoof's Old Town: 1795 circa, the village of Shawnee Principal Chief Black Hoof (Puckinswa - Puck'IN -swa)

Blue Creek People: The Eski'seppi Naube (Eskee' ceepee Nau'bee Algonquian) or the Talig'wah (Toweleeg'waah) are a very private Shawnee community comprised of Fort Ancient, Raven and Scioto sects of southern Ohio prehistoric mound builder Indians. Today they are known as Shawnee because of the alliance with the Shawnee in the 1600's

Blue River Community: Panji'Seepe Naube (Paangee'Seepee Nau'bee) an ancient Shawnee community originally located on the banks of Blue Creek in northern Indiana. They are descendents of Paughp (Paoughp) or Thick Water, who was Tecumseh's first cousin, best friend, first warrior, and personal body guard. After the death of Tecumseh in 1813 Thick Water and his band retired to Blue River. Many of the Shawnee United Remnant Band, including Paugph's grandson, Principal Chief Hawk Pope are descendents of this community.

Bundle: A Bundle is as the word implies, an assemblage of items that are traditionally wrapped in an animal hide or hides and/or wooden boxes. Other wraps and containers can also used. There are many different kinds of Bundles, tribal, personal, medicine, burial, etc. To the Shawnee the Bundle contains a "table of contents" of the spirituality of that People. The items in these Bundles are not in themselves Sacred, but are artifacts and materials of great significance that remind the owner of the responsibilities of being an Indian. Within the Bundle are all the items needed to perform the ceremonies of the Shawnee.

Changing His Feathers, Penagashega: 1796-1803 *n.* (P?nägä'sheegah *Changing His Feathers* Algonquian- Wakashan) Spiritual Leader or Shaman of the Chalagawtha Sept of the Shawnee People,

Named Tecumseh from the omen of the meteorite that crossed the sky at his birth, "The eye of the Panther" or "Panther in the Sky,"

Charnel House: *n* (Chr'n'l) OFr. *Charnel* - LL. *carnale* a building or place where corpses and bones are deposited or piled up, a burial house for prehistoric Indians of the eastern United States where corpses were left to decay and later the bones were assembled and wrapped for the final journey into dust.

chena: *conj.* (chea'nah *and* Algonquian- Wakashan) the equivalent of the English, and.

Cherokee: *n* (Cher'ah kee tribal name Tsah'rahgee, probably from the Choctaw chiluk'ki, "cave people") member of a tribe of Iroquoian Indians originally from the eastern United States most of whom were removed to Okalahoma in the Trail of Tears in the early 1800's. the largest of the Indian nations today, descendants of the eastern mound builders.

Chief Seattle: *n* (See-aatl) originally Seatlh. 1786?–1866, Duwamish, Suquamish, and allied peoples Native American leader, who befriended white settlers of the Pacific Northwest. The city of Seattle is named for him.

Chief Ten Moons Watters: *n* Metathwe Dekeelswa (Meath'ahth wee *tenth* Dee'k?yl swah *moons* Algonquian- Wakashan) 1904–1993, Shawnee Blue Creek Community Chief, Chief and Elder of the Shawnee Nation United Remnant Band, educator, journalist, author, artist, entertainer, labor activist and Journeyman Ironworker. Served with honors in the US Army horse drawn artillery in WWI and as a Navy SeeBee in WWII.

Chief Way: to do as the Chief says, or in the manner of a Chief.

Chownumnee: *n.* (Chow'nu mnee) Sierra Nevada Native American Tribe, related to the Mono People.

Chukchanse: *n.* Sierra Nevada Native American Tribe, related to the Mono People.

Circle of Life: the Sacred Hoop of Native American spiritualism signifying that all things are related, that all things are important in our lives.

Clan: *n,* a division of a tribe tracing descent from a common ancestor. a large group of relatives, friends, or associates.

Coashellaqua: *n* (Cooahshee' lah quah *Great Black Mystery* Algonquian- Wakashan) the name of the faith of the Woodland Shawnee handed down by the Blue River Community, a monotheistic religion based on a belief in the Great Black Mystery that created by thought the earth and the sky and all things between, a faith that holds sacred the trinity of Gieclamookalong (Geeslah 'mookah long Algonquian), Kiji Manito (Kee'gee Mahnah too Algonquian), and Nanabusho (Nahnah boo' shoa Algonquian)

Council: *n* a body of advisers to a head of state, the governing body of an Indian Tribe, in ancient times there were men's and women's Councils that governed separately on matters of the gender and collectively on matters of state, the Shawnee Nation United Remnant Band Council is comprised of co-equal male and female representatives of the Twelve Clans, Elders on Council, and Moon Society who each have one equal vote. In addition there are male and female representatives on Council for Allied Tribes, Youth Council, Friends of the People Society who act in an advisory capacity.

Creator: *n* the name Native American's use for their Deity, the Supreme being or God, other various names given are Gieclamookalong,the Great Manitou or Kiji Manito, and Nanabusho and the Great Black Mystery, *He Who Creates With Thought.*

Creek / Muskogea: n (kreek): a Native American people formerly inhabiting eastern Alabama, southwest Georgia, and northwest Florida and now located in central Oklahoma and southern Alabama. The Creek were removed to Indian Territory in the 1830s. a member of this people. the n (Mus-kougeen) language of the Creek. A Native American confederacy made up of the Creek and various smaller southeast tribes. a member of this confederacy. In all senses also called Muskogee(Mus-kougee <maaskóoki. Creek)..

Dakota: *adj & n* (Dah·ko·tah Siouan) any of the Sioux peoples, especially any of the peoples of the Santee branch. a member of a Sioux people, especially a Santee. the Siouan language of the Dakota, especially the dialect of the Santee.

Dance Arena: *n* an area that has been blessed and is designated for dancing and ceremonies at a powwow.

dekeelswa: *n* (de'keyl swah Algonquian- Wakashan) the moon(s).

dream catcher: *n* variously named Asubakacin (Asooba' kiasin Ojibwe - White Earth Band - *net-like, looks like a net*) and Bwaajige Ngwaagan (Bwah'jgeh Ngwah'jgeh   Ojibwe - Curve Lake Band - *dream snare*) hoop made of willow with sinew or string woven in the circle to replicate a spiders web. for children, 3.not meant to last. made by Native American artists from many Nations. Ojibwe (called Chippewa by others) originated the dream catcher. said to catch and hold everything evil as a spider's web catches and holds everything that comes into contact with it, only lets goodness fall down upon the person below.

Earth Mother: *n* Native American phrase to show reverence to the Gift of Creator, the earth.

Earth People: *n.* Reference to Indian relationship to the earth, a widely held belief that we came from the earth

Elders: *n* 1. an older person. an older, influential member of a family, tribe, or community.

elene: *n* (eah'lehneh *man* Algonquian- Wakashan) Male, man, men

Eski'seppi Naube: *n* ('skee' *ceepee blue creek*, Nau'p? *nation,* Algonquian- Wakashan) Blue Creek Nation of Mound Builder People

Ezine: *n* Contemporary slang for an email magazine.

Fall Council: *n* Major meeting of a woodland tribe usually held in September or October, sometimes held in conjunction with Fall Harvest Celebration.

Feather Flag: *n.* Native American equivalent to a nation's flag, usually a staff or "shepherd's crook" with many honor feathers. Spiritual symbol for many Indian People.

Fiat: *n.* (Feeaht) Fiat is an acronym for Fabbrica Italiana Automobili Torino, which, literally translated, means Italian Automobile Factory of Turin, a Turin Italian automotive manufacturer founded in 1899.

First Parents: *n.* reference to the first humans created by the Deity, Creator.

First People: *n.* same as first parents

Fort Ancient / Fort Ancient culture: *n.* (A.D. 1000 -1650) thrived along the Ohio River watershed in southern Ohio and northern Kentucky, villages were made up of a number of circular or rectangular houses surrounding an open plaza, their descendents are the many woodland Native Americans most predominately the Shawnee Blue Creek and Raven Community and today's Shawnee Nation United Remnant Band.

Geah: *n.* (gee'ah *mother* Algonquian- Wakashan) mother, female leader, female Chief.

Gieclamookalong: *n.* (Geeslah 'mookah long *Great Black Mystery* Algonquian- Wakashan), Supreme Deity, God.

Grandmother Turtle: *n.* Eastern woodland Indian traditional folk hero, the animal person who went to the bottom of the water to retrieve mud from which Creator made the earth, called the Great Turtle Island or North America.

grandparents grandparents: *phrase* term used by Indian storytellers to indicate that the story took place a very long time in the past.

Great Circle: *n.* see Circle of Life.

Great Council Lodge / Grand Council Lodge: *n.* Building used for international meetings of many Indian Nations in North America.

Great Spirit: *n.* Native American name for God.

Great Turtle Island: *n.* North America, the land made from the mud retrieve from the bottom of the waters, See Grandmother Turtle.

Great White Father: *n.* Native America term for the President of the United States, King of England (and Canada), King of France, a derogatory term for oppressive presidents or kings.

Green Corn Ceremony: *n.* Native American harvest ceremony celebrated by the Shawnee, Creek, Cherokee, Seminole, Yuchi, and Iroquois Indians and other tribes, held during the full moon when the first corn crop is ready for harvest, the date depends on the growth of the corn. a time of thanksgiving for the crops and forgiveness of old grudges, the first days of the ceremony are known as the Busk when people fast, clean their homes and their selves to purify everything, then the corn is harvested, followed with dancing, singing, playing, and feasting.

Ground Zero: *n. 1.* term given to the site of the Twin Towers in New York City after they were destroyed by terrorist on September 11, 2001.

Handsome Lake: *n.*(Seneca 1735?–1815), Seneca religious prophet; half brother of *Cornplanter*. After a long illness he had a vision (c. 1800) and began to preach new religious beliefs. His moral teachings showed a similarity to Christian ethics and had a profound effect among the Iroquois. He advocated giving up the nomadic Native American life in favor of agriculture, much to the disgust of *Red Jacket*. Though Christian missionaries opposed Handsome Lake's religion, it nevertheless persisted alongside Christianity. "Handsome Lake" from The Factmonster Dictionary. © 2000 Learning Network. http://www.factmonster.com/ipd/A0515599. html (November 21, 2001).

Harvey, Paul: Politically conservative radio and TV commentator.

Hoh / Hoh River Indians: *n.* (tribal name - Chimaquan)*1.* considered a band of the Quileutes but are recognized as a separate tribe. reservation consists of 443 acres located 28 miles south of Forks, and 80 miles north of Aberdeen, Washington, the Hoh Indian Reservation was established 9/11/1963 and has a formal Tribal

Hopi: *n.* (Hoh'pee *peaceable* Hopi-Uto-Aztecan) A Pueblo people occupying a number of mesa-top pueblos on reservation land in northeast Arizona. The Hopi are noted for their dry-farming techniques, rich ceremonial life, and craftsmanship in basketry, pottery, silverwork, and weaving. a member of this people, the Uto-Aztecan language of the Hopi.

Indian Way: Native American term meaning to do in a manner consistent with Indian traditions and cultures

Iron Eyes Cody: *n.* (Cherokee) famous Native American actor, 1904-1999; most known for the "Keep America Beautiful" commercial where he sheds a tear in disbelief at his fouled native land; layed many other Indian characters, including roles in "Sitting Bull," "Paleface," and "A Man Called Horse." An accomplished Indian dancer and Indian hand signing. Cody is survived by his son Robert Tree, three grandchildren, and a niece.

Iroquois: *n.* (Eer'oh-kuwoy' *Real Adders* Algonquian- Wakashan) a Native American confederacy inhabiting New York State and originally composed of the Mohawk, Oneida, Onondaga, Cayuga, and Seneca peoples, known as the Five Nations. After 1722 the confederacy was joined by the Tuscaroras to form the Six Nations. Also called *Iroquois League.* a member of this confederacy or of any of its peoples. Any or all of the languages of the Iroquois.

Ishi: *n.* (Ee'shee, *man* – Yahi-Hokan) 1860? – 1916) known as the "Last Wild Indian" from the Yahi Tribe of the Southern Yani Nation in California. Attributed to be of the Hokan superfamily of North America. Ishi working with two professors of anthropology at the University of California, Alfred L. Kroeber and T. T. Waterman spent the last five years of his life documenting his culture for posterity.

Ivaluarjuk, Iglulik or Iglulingmiut: *n.* (Ehvahlooer' jook Ehvahlook Ehvahlookoung'mm-oht *People of the Snow House Place* Inuktitut-Eskimo-Aleut [Athapaskan]) Principal band of the Iglulik Tribe, the people refer to themselves as Iglulingmiut , one of eight cultural groups northeast Artic Canadian Inuit or Eskimo groups residing in the Nunavut Provence.

Kansans: *n* (Kahn'sahn *People of the south wind* Siouian) Central Plains Indians related the Omaha'ian group.

Kepish: *n* (Kaep'eash *with face hair* Algonquian-Wakashan) mud-puppy, salamander, any of various small lizard-like amphibians of the order Caudata, having porous scaleless skin and four, often weak or rudimentary legs.

Kiji Manito: *n.* (Kee'gee Mahnah too   *Great Spirit*   Algonquian-Wakashan),   God

kindewa sawagateah: *n.* (kindeh' waeh sah'waehgah'teh aeh Algonquian-Wakashan) Eagle feathers

Kitch Okeama: *n.* (Kitch, Okee'mah Algonquian-Wakashan) *1.* Great Chief or Great Leader.

Kiwanis: *n.* (keewah´nis   *to make oneself known*   *keewanis* Algonquian-Wakashan)   community service organization of business and professional people, founded in 1915 at Detroit, Mich. Local Kiwanis clubs meet weekly, each local Kiwanis club has a voice in Kiwanis International, which is organized throughout the United States and Canada.

Kohkumthena: *n.* (Kohkoum'thenah Algonquian-Wakashan) female Supreme Deity, Grandmother God, God, the pair-deity with Manitimussumtha.

Lakota: *n* (Lah koh tah *considered friend* Siouian) also known as the Santee Sioux, members of the family of the Great Sioux Nation of North America, prehistorically the largest of the three main Siouian groups originally from the upper Mississippi watershed in what is now Minnesota.

Lenni Lanape: (Laeneh Lahnaupee   *True People, Old Men or Grandfathers* Algonquian-Wakashan) a group of closely related Native American peoples formerly inhabiting the Delaware and Hudson river valleys and the area between, with present-day populations in Oklahoma, Kansas, Wisconsin, and Ontario. The Delaware formed a variety of political alliances in their westward migration after losing their lands to white settlement in the 17th and 18th centuries. a member of a Delaware people. Also called *Lenape,* one or both of the Algonquian languages of the Delaware. The Delaware People.

Little Fog's Vision: (992 A.D.) Little Fog was a Shawandasse Bear Walker and shaman for the People when they lived along the banks of Lake Chapalla in central Mexico. The predominate culture of the Toltecs had enslaved the Lenni Lanape (Shawnee ancestors) and used them in sacrifices. in 992 Little Fog had a vision that called for the People to leave Mexico and return to the homeland where the wall of ice had driven them south so many generations before. Little Fog led twenty thousand Lenni Lanape and assorted bands east and north to eventually settle in the homelands of the Appalachian Mountains and it's watershed.

Longknives: *n.* Indian name for the European and American military, given because of their side swords, derogatory name for whites.

Lumbee: *n.* (lum'bee, regional slang for lumber) a 40,000+ Native American Tribe of southeast North Carolina. a member of this people, the largest tribe in North Carolina, the largest tribe east of the Mississippi River and the ninth largest in the nation. the Lumbee take their name from the Lumbee River, the ancestors of the Lumbee were mainly Cheraw and related Siouan-speaking Indians who have lived in the area since the 1700s. the Lumbee people have been recognized by the state of North Carolina since 1885, in 1956 a bill was passed by the United States Congress which recognized the Lumbee as Indian, but denied the tribe full status as a federally recognized Indian tribe. Federal recognition for the tribe is currently being sought through federal legislation.

Mana' hu: *interj.* a greeting in Mono

Manitimussumtha: *n* (Mahnehteah' mousoumthah *our Grandfather that is the sky* Algonquian) Sky Grandfather, God, the pair-deity with Kohkumthena

Manito, Manitou: *n.* (Mahnah too Algonquian) God, a Deity

Makwa: n. (mah'quah Algonquian-Wakashan) Bear.

Mardi Gras: *n.*(mardee grah French : *mardi gras*, Fat Tuesday from the feasting on Mardi Gras before Lenten fasting). Shrove Tuesday, celebrated as a holiday in many places with carnivals, masquerade balls, and parades of costumed merrymakers, a carnival period coming to a climax on this day, an occasion of great festivity and merrymaking,

Master of Life: *n.* Shawnee name for God.

Matchemonito: n. (Mahchee Mahnah too *the Evil One* Algonquian-Wakashan) the opposite of the Great Spirit Kiji Manito, Created when the Great Manito saw it's reflection in the water and wondered what that was, therefore creating by thought the exact opposite of Creator.

Medicine Way: Native American term relating to living in a prescribed spiritual manner.

Medicine Wheel: *n.* a spiritual circle or site used by Native American spiritual leaders for certain ceremonies.

Megwich: *interj.* (meag' wch Algonquian-Wakashan) I thank you, I am thankful.

Meswammi Pitchkosan: *n.*(maes' waehmee ptchkousahn Algonquian-Wakashan) Sacred Treasures.

Metathwe: *n* (meht'vhf wee Algonquian-Wakashan) numeral ten (10)

Mide', Mide'wiian Midewiwin society: *n.* (maeday'wee'in, *Great Black Magic* Algonquian-Wakashan) Ojibway spiritual and medicine practice, Southern Ohio Talig'wah (Shawnee) mound builder spiritual and medicine practice of understanding all things in the four levels of both earth and sky, in order to be prepared for the afterlife, sacred rituals and prayers.

Moon, Crackling: *n.* Ohio Mide' term for the eleventh full moon in the Shawnee-Mide' calendar, in the calendar month of January, so called because or the crackling sound of the hard ice compressing.

Moon, First Snow: *n.* Ohio Mide' term for the tenth full moon in the Shawnee-Mide' calendar, usually in December, as it's name implies the time when the first snow fall that stays, sometimes given to the time the snow actually falls regardless of the time of year.

Moon, Harvest: *n.* Ohio Mide' term for the seventh full moon in the Shawnee-Mide' calendar, usually in September, as it's name implies, it is the full moon at the time of harvest.

Moon, Red Paint: *n.* Ohio Mide' term for the fourth full moon in the Shawnee-Mide' calendar, usually in July, a moon that is red in color because of dust in the air.

Mono: *n.* (Wau-Dau-Sa-Ah *Band of the* Nuem group) name of the Western Mono, San Joaquin or Big Sandy Band, ancestral home or village sites in the Auberry, California area. On Big Sandy Rancheria there are 30 home sites which include homes of tribal members.

M'tekwaw: *n.* (mtahk'waawh *Eagle People* Algonquian-Wakashan) Ohio Mide' name for eagles, the oral traditional animal hero who carried the tree's message to Creator.

M'tekyah: *n.* (mtahk'yeah *Tree People* Algonquian-Wakashan) Ohio Mide' name for trees, the oral traditional plant person who wished to commune with Creator.

Nanabusho: *n.* (Nahnah boo' shoa *the Trickster* Algonquian-Wakashan) name of one of the trinity of Spirits of the Shawnee-Mide' religious practices, the Spiritual aspect of Creation that "feels" our emotions, the Spiritual aspect that is closest to humans.

Nappe: *n.* (Nauh'pee Algonquian-Wakashan) water.

Narragansett: *n.* (nar'eh gahn'set *on a cape* Algonquian) NE tribe of Indians who lived around Narragansett Bay, RI.

Navaho, Navajo: *n.* (Nahveh'ho *great fields* Tewa) largets Indian Nation in the United States, they call themselves the Dineh or simply the People.

nekah: *n.* (neh'kay Algonquian-Wakashan) friend or comrade.

New Ones: reference to the humans in difference to the animals and plants and minerals that the Great Spirit had Created.

ni, mi: *poss adj.* (neh, meh *my* Algonquian-Wakashan) ni - masculine for my as in "my friend, mi - feminine, i.e. niNekah (my friend).

niSooos pëh: *n.* (niehSooz paeh Algonquian-Wakashan) I love you, soos - romantic love.

Nishnas Chantoon: (Nehshnahsh Chahntoon *the People speak* Algonquian-Wakashan) term used to describe the voice of the general populace of the Shawnee Nation United Remnant Band.

Ogallala: *n.* (ogha' la la *to scatter one's own* Siouxian) one of the several Sioux Indian Nations.

okeama: *n* (oh'keemeh *chief or leader* Algonquian-Wakashan)

Onondaga: *n.* (Ahnohn'dahgah *hill People* Iroquoian) one of the five Iroquoian tribes that compose the Five Nations or the Iroquian Confederacy, now known as the Six Nations Confederacy located in upper state New York.

Oraibi: *n* (Orib) N Arizona pueblo built c.1150 on a mesa N of Winslow, for hundreds of years it was the most important pueblo of the *Hopi,* but because of economic and internal discord inhabitants left in 1907 to form the pueblos of Bakavi and Hotevila, now it is a ruin.

Paughp: n. (paugh'p *thick water* Algonquian-Wakashan) Thick Water eventually became anglicizes into Pope

Pipe Presenter: a person who presents the ceremonial pipe to others in a Native American pipe ceremony.

Pottawatomie: *n.* (pautah'wahtoh'mee *People of the Place of the Fire* Algonquian-Wakashan) Great Lakes Algonquian Indian tribe, traditional Keepers of the Sacred Fire.

powwow: *n.* Native American gathering.

Prager, Dennis: one of America's most respected thinkers, Dennis Prager is an author, lecturer, teacher, and theologian with a nationally syndicated radio talk show originating from Los Angeles.

Pueblo: *n.* (p'wehb' low Spanish) any of some 25 Native American peoples, including the Hopi, Zuñi, and Taos, living in established villages in northern and western New Mexico and northeast Arizona. The Pueblo are considered to be descendants of the cliff-dwelling Anasazi peoples and are noted for their skilled craft in pottery, basketry, weaving, and metalworking. a member of any of these peoples. pueblo Inflected forms: pl. pueb·los A permanent village or community of any of the Pueblo peoples, typically consisting of multilevel adobe or stone apartment dwellings of terraced design clustered around a central plaza.

Quest of Solitude: a spiritual journey to find a place where one can pray and meditate without interruption.

Ramadan: *n.* (Rahmahdehn *to be scorched* Arabic) the ninth month of the year in the Islamic calendar, a fast, held from sunrise to sunset, that is carried out during this period.

Red Man: *n.* term used to describe the American Indian, a derogatory ethnic slur, believed to have originated in the 1500's when the first European explorers met the American Indians who painted their bodies with red ochre, these people were inhabitants of the north east coast of what is now the United States.

Red Road: *n. a* term used by the plains Indians and much of the rest of Indian Country to describe a spiritual path, refers to a portion of the plains Indian spiritual practice of the peyote based religion, the "good" road to be on in your Indian life.

Rosh Hashana: *n.* (Rohsh' hah'shawnah lit. *head of the New Year* Hebrew) Jewish New year.

Sachem, sachimau: *n.* (saehchehm, saehchehmoh *chief or spiritual leader* Algonquian-Wakashan) Native American tribal leader, leader of a confederacy, spiritual society leaders.

Sampa: *n.* (sahm'pah Algonquian-Wakashan) the Sacred Tobacco used by the Shawnee for their prayer ceremonies.

Seasons of the Many Deaths: Another term for winter.

Seneca: *n.* (ahsinea' keah *People of the Standing Rock* Mohegan translation of the Iroquois oneh'niute' roh'n non) one of the five Iroquoian tribes that compose the Five Nations or the Iroquian Confederacy, now known as the Six Nations Confederacy located in upper state New York.

Seppe: *n* (see'pee Algonquian-Wakashan) *1.* river or stream.

Sertoma: Sertoma International Founded in 1912 in Kansas City, Mo., volunteer civic service organization with about men and women in 830 Clubs in the United States, Canada and Mexico. Sertoma stands for SERvice TO MAnkind. provides service to people with speech and hearing disorders,projects that promote freedom and democracy, youth causes, and other local community

Seven Generations: a Native American designation to indicate that we are connected to and responsible for our actions to all things as long ago as the seven generations that preceded us, and to the next seven generations not yet born.

Shaman: *n.* (sha'mahn *spiritual leader* Tungusic) Asian or American Indian priest, monk or medicine man who practices shamanism, a belief based on good and evil spirits.

Shape-Shifter: *n.* (plains Indians) a Native American spiritual leader that is trained to invoke supernatural powers, able to transport oneself to other places by the use of the power of thought, a Bear Walker.

Shawandasse, Shawnee: n. (shah'wahn *South Wind*, dahcee' *People of the*, *sha'wan?* Algonquian-Wakasian) the name that the Shawnee call themselves, Southern People, People from the south, Great Lakes Algonquian tribe.

Shawnee Nation United Remnant Band (SNURB): a state recognized tribe, one of the major bands of Shawnee centered in Ohio, the band of Shawnee who are descendents of the followers of Tecumseh and their families.

Sioux: *n.* (Sue *snakes, or enemy* North American French short for nadouéssioux, from Ojibway naadowesiwag) a group of Native American peoples, also known as the Dakota, inhabiting the northern Great Plains from Minnesota to eastern Montana and from southern Saskatchewan to Nebraska. Present-day Sioux populations are located mainly in North and South Dakota. a member of any of these peoples. Any of the Siouan languages of the Sioux peoples.

Sky People: Mide' religious term, refers to all the animals and elements that make up the area above the surface of the earth, but does not include plants growing from the surface.

Smugging, Smugged: the act of using smoke from sacred herbs to purify and cleanse oneself for ceremonies, widespread among most North American Indian people.

Soroptimist: a world wide organization for women in management and the professions formed in 1921, The organization strives for human rights for all, equality, development and peace through international goodwill and understanding and friendship. Soroptimist International is committed to service to local, national and international communities, active participation in decision making at all levels of society.

Spaylaywitheepi: *n.*(spalah'wehtheepee Algonquian-Wakashan) Ohio River.

Speaker: *n.* person who is designated to speak for others, an important and wise person, one who is known as a Speaker.

Spirit Dancers: *n.* super-natural beings that dance messages in dreams ans at special times for Native American's on a Bear Walk or a vision quest, spirits that inform shaman and medicine people.

Spirits Guides: *n.* super-natural beings that guide Native American's on a vision quest.

Stickys: *n.* yellow adhesive backed note papers, 3M Post-it note paper.

Stone Pipe: *n.* Ceremonial or personal pipe used for Sacred prayers by American Indians.

Storyteller: *n.* keeper of the oral tradition, a teacher that brings their message through parables and stories.

Sweat Lodge: *n.* the most often used form of sweat lodge among American Indians is the hot rock system, usually used native people in the central plains, the southwest, the Great Basin and parts of the eastern woodlands. They can be permanent, portable, or temporary and are smaller than the domed and/or oblong native homes. They can be covered with logs, bark, blankets or skins and some permanent ones are made of mud or sod. Steam for the sweat is made by sprinkling hot rocks with water. Although simple in design, every detail is a spiritual representation.

Tadodaho: *n.* (tahdoh'dah'hoh Iroquois) Fire Keeper, position of the greatest honor, League speaker, Wisdom Keeper.

Talig'wah: *n.* (thaehleeg'wah *of the earth* pre-Aogonquian) one of the five septs of the Shawnee comprised of descendents of the Thalegiwa-Hathawekila Ft. Ancient Mound builders that joined the Shawnee Confederacy in the 1100's.

Tanakia: *vt.* (taehnah'keeah *thank you* Algonquian-Wakashan) *1.* to express appreciation.

Tecumseh: *n.* (The'kumseeah *Panther in the Sky* Algonquian-Wakashan) , b 1768? Clark Co., Ohio – d 1813 Ontario Canada., War Chief of the Shawnee,.Among his people he became distinguished for his prowess in battle, but he opposed the practice of torturing prisoners. When the United States refused to recognize his principle that all Native American land was the common possession of all the Native Americans and that land could not rightly be ceded by, or purchased from, an individual tribe, Tecumseh set out to bind together the Native Americans of the Old Northwest Territory, the South, and the eastern Mississippi valley. His plan failed with the defeat of his brother, the Shawnee Prophet, at Tippecanoe (1811). Though Tippecanoe was, properly speaking, a drawn battle, it marked the collapse of the Native American military movement. In the War of 1812, Tecumseh allied himself with the British and was made a brigadier general. He led a large force of Native Americans in the siege of Fort Meigs, covered Gen. Henry Procter's retreat after the American victory on Lake Erie, and lost his life in the battle of the Thames (see Thames, battle of the), in which Gen. William Henry Harrison overwhelmed Procter and his Native American allies. Tecumseh had great ability as an organizer and a leader and is considered one of the outstanding Native Americans in American history.

Tekonsha: *n.* (Teh'koahn shah *cornstalk* Algonquian-Wakashan) Major Shawnee Chief and war chief, Chief Cornstalk 1743 circa - 1777.

Thorpe, Jim: *n.* (Wa tho' huk, *Bright Path* Algonquian-Wakashan) 1887b–1953d. Sac and Fox Indian with a small French and Irish heritage, legendary Native American athlete acclaimed to be the greatest athlete of the 20th Century, Thorpe excelled in virtually every major athletic event available.

Torah: n. (Taou' rauh *law* Hebrew) in the broadest sense the body of G_d's teaching or guidance revealed to Israel, the Jewish people, the first five books of the Hebrew Scriptures, the Bible. a scroll of parchment containing the first five books of the Hebrew Scriptures, used in a synagogue during services. the entire body of religious law and learning including both sacred literature and oral tradition.

Tukemas: *n.* (too'keemahs *Hawk at the Setting Sun* Algonquian-Wakashan) 1941b- *1.* Hawk Pope, Principal Chief of the Shawnee Nation United Remnant Band since 1970, 2. Keeper of the Tradition of the Shawnee Blue River People.

Tula: *n.*(too'lah *earth* Algonquian-Wakashan) the earth, soil, of the earth, of Grandmother Earth.

Turtle Mountain: *n.* located in north central North Dakota, with Canada bordering the north. home to the Turtle Mountain Band of Chippewa. reservation school

Tuscarora: n. (Tous'keuh roarah, *hemp gatherers* Iroquoian) a Native American people formerly inhabiting parts of North Carolina, with present-day populations in western New York and southeast Ontario, Canada. The Tuscarora migrated northward in the 18th century, joining the Iroquois confederacy in 1722 and adopting aspects of the Iroquois culture, a member of this people, the Iroquoian language of the Tuscarora.

two-legged: Human, man

Valley of Darkness: in the oral tradition of the woodland Indians, before there was light, all People lived in this valley where there was no light.

wapiti: *n.* (wahpeht'ee *white rump* Algonquian-Wakasan) a large light brown or grayish-brown North American deer (Cervus canadensis) having long, branching antlers, <u>elk</u>, also called <u>American Elk</u>,

Wee-lo: *v.* (wea'loh   Algonquian-Wakasan) *find, I found,* call to Creator when a human body is found.

Woodland People: *n.* name used to identify Native Americans who's tribes originated in the eastern United States. Indian Tribes that lived in the woods east of the Mississippi.

yerba santa: *n* ('urbah sahn teh Spanish) any of various western North American evergreen shrubs of the genus *Eriodictyon,* having purple or white flowers borne in coiled cymes and a funnel-shaped corolla.

Yom Kipper: *n.* (yahm kaeh'poo'r *the Day of Atonement* Hebrew) a Jewish holy day observed on the tenth day of Tishri in September or October when nothing is eaten all day and people say prayers in the synagogue asking for forgiveness for things they have done wrong.

Zonta: n. (zhoan'tah *"honest and trustworthy."* Lakota/Sioux) Zonta International is a worldwide service organization of executives in business and the professions working together to advance the status of women. There are over 34,000 members in more than 1,230 clubs in 70 countries. founded in 1919 in Buffalo, New York, USA, Zonta takes its name from the Lakota Sioux Indian word meaning "honest and trustworthy." Zontians volunteer their time, talents and energy to local and international service projects.

Zuni: n. (Zoo'nee the Zuni call themselves Ashiwi *the people* Zuñian) a pueblo people located in western New Mexico. a member of this people. the language of the Zuni, of no known linguistic affiliation.

The American Heritage® Dictionary of the English Language – online 4th edition.

Selected Bibliography

Books:

American Indian Artifacts—How to Identify, Evaluate and Care for Your Collection. °1997 Seven Locks Press. ISBN 0-929765-55-9

Archeological History of Ohio—The Mound Builders and Later Indians. Gerard Fowke 1902, The Ohio State Archeological and Historical Society.

At One with All Life. °1989 Dr. Judith Boice, Findhorn Press. ISBN 0-905249-74-7

Black Elk Speaks. John G. Neihardt °1932,1959,1972 ©1961 by the John G. Neihardt Trust, Bison Book Edition—University of Nebraska Press. ISBN 0-8032-8359-8

Chautauqua. Timm Severeud °1990-96, *Chautauqua Ezine—Echoes in the Wind.*

Chicken Soup for the Soul. (the series) Mark Hansen and Jack Canfield Health Communications, Inc.

Creation's Journey-Native American Identity and Belief. (A must-read—for anyone who wants to understand Indian thinking.) Tom Hill (Seneca) and Richard Hill, Sr., (Tuscarora) °1994 Smithsonian Institute books, ISBN 1-560098-455-8

Fools Crow—Wisdom and Power. °1991 Council Oaks Books. ISBN 0-933031-35-1

Indian Givers. °1988 Fawcett Columbine Book Published by Ballantine Books. ISBN 0-449-90496-2

Inherit the Blood—Poetry and Fiction. Barney Bush (Must-read—Shawnee) ©1985 Thunder's Mouth Press. ISBN 0-938410-28-8

Ishi In Two Worlds. Theodora Kroeber ©1961 University of California Press. ISBN 0-520-00675-5

Jimmie's Place. Cora Munn Tula Watters ©2000 Tula's Lodge Publishing, 696 Blacks Run Rd., Lynx, OH 45650.

Kohkumthena's Grandchildren The Shawnee. (Must-read—Hard-core Ohio era Shawnee traditions.) Dark Rain Thom ©1994 Guild Press of Indiana, Inc. ISBN 1-878208-53-29-5

Panther in the Sky. (Must-read—If you want to really understand what Shawnee life was during the invasions.) James Alexander Thom ©1989 Ballantine Books. ISBN 0-345-36638-7

Stick Around. Paul Helzer ©1995 Self-Published, 9461 Flower Street, Bellflower, CA 90706. ISBN 0-9651607-0-x

Staying Put—Making a Home in a Restless World. (The book that focused my journey in writing) Scott Russell Sanders ©1993 Beacon Press. ISBN 0-8070-6341-x

The Art of Daily Activism. Dr. Judith Boice ©1992 Wingbow Press. ISBN 0914728-74-1

The Children Of First Man. (Must-Read—Astounding concept on early visitors to the Great Turtle Island.) James Alexander Thom ©1994 Ballantine Books. ISBN 0-345-37005-8.

The Mother Earth—Through the Eyes of Women. Dr. Judith Boice ©1993 Sierra Club Books. ISBN 0-87156-456-4.

Think a Second Time. Dennis Prager ©1995 Regan Books, an imprint of HarperCollins Publishers. ISBN 0-06-039157-x

Through Indian Eyes. (Must-read—A well-source reference on Indian life.)—Readers' Digest General Books ©1995 The Reader's Digest Association ISBN 0-89577-819-x

Viscott, Dr. David. (For a balanced approach to better living, whether you be Indian or other, anything by this psychiatrist.) Pocket Books, a Division of Simon and Schuster, Inc.

Wisdom Keepers. (Must-read—This is the bible of Indian-ness for me) Steve Wall and Harvey Arden ©1990 Beyond Words Publishing, Inc. ISBN 0-941831-55-8

Art, Music, Periodicals, and Websites:

Note: I urge you to explore the Iinternet for topics on Indian-ness, but, first, a CAVEAT . . . there is precious little about Indians that can be authenticated on the Web. Read, but verify. So many on the Internet are very angry people who live in denial as to the reality of the Indian today. There are agendas and outright lies, but there are also many worthy sites that it is in your best interest to search them out. I will post recommended sites on my Web-page as I sift them from the chaff.

"May your hunt be fruitful and your belly full."
Chief Hawk Pope's Art Gallery. (View our past in images conceived from the soul of this extraordinary artist.) http://shawneeurb.homestead.com/Gallery.html or contact Chief Hawk Pope, 2911 St. Elmo Pl., Middletown, OH 45042.

Earth Spirit. (or anything Nakai has produced) R. Carlos Nakai ©1987 Canyon Records Productions CD-612 Vol. 4.

Honor the Earth Powwow—Songs of the Great Lakes Indians. ©1991 360' Publishing—Rykodisk RCD 10199.

Remake of the American Dream. (A great selection of Shawnee-Blue

River music. Best bet to find a copy is to contact Chief Hawk Pope: 2911 St. Elmo Pl., Middletown, OH 45042.) Tony Hymas, Barney Bush and the Shawnee Nation United Remnant Band Drum, ©1992 Nato Records, Paris, France DK 018-53012-2.

Spirit—A Journey in Dance, Drum and Song. (This should be available on order, or contact Chief Hawk Pope: 2911 St. Elmo Pl., Middletown, OH 45042) ©1999 Uni/Hollywood; ASIN B00000I608.

Periodicals:

American Indian. ©1999-2001 Smithsonian's National Museum of the American Indian. ISSN 1528-0640, USPS 019-246.

Native Peoples. ©1990-2001 Media Concepts Publications, Inc. for the National Museum of the American Indian Smithsonian Institute. ISSN 0895-7606.

National Geographic Magazine. You know the magazine. It is a continuing well-source of great information on Indians.

Tosan. (The longest continuing Native American Newspaper in the nation. contact: Chief Hawk Pope 2911 St. Elmo Pl., Middletown, OH 45042.) Chief Hawk Pope ©1975-2001 Shawnee Nation United Remnant Band.

Websites:

Chief Jim Great Elk Waters: www.home.earthlink.net/~kijiwaters/

Dennis Prager: http://www.dennisprager.com/ (For a non-Indian, he has a good understanding of what it means to be Indian. Perhaps it is because of his Jewish heritage.)

Dr. Judith Boice: www.Drjudithboice.com

eh'dasse: http://www.ehdasse.com/welcome.htm

Spirit—A Journey in Dance, Drum and Song: www.Spiritdance.com

Zane Shawnee Caverns & Woodland Native American Museum: http://www.homestead.com/zaneshawneecaverns/introduction.html

Index